Broken Spirits:

A letter to my cousin, Rodney G. King,
A Memoir

by
Ontresicia Averette
and
Michele L. Waters

Crystall Clear$P$ublishing

www.crystallclearpublishing.com

Broken Spirits: A Letter to My Cousin, Rodney G. King
A Memoir

Crystall Clear Publishing

ISBN – 978-0-9828670-2-0
ISBN – 0982867026

Crystall Clear Publishing
25379 Wayne Pl Suite # 193
Valencia, CA. 91355

www.crystallclearpublishing.com
www.michelelwaters.com

Book Cover design by:
www.mariondesigns.com

Special Thanks

I want to thank Michele L. Waters for believing in me enough to take on this writing project and Nikki Richards, our publicist for all of her great promotions and marketing skills.

I have a host of siblings and cousins that I'd like to thank for allowing me to be a part of their lives: Douglas, Juline, and Earl who are my siblings. I thank my cousins Debra, Sandra, Marcia, Laurie, Juanita, Daphne, and Ondre who all taught me how to be a big sister to everyone else in our family younger than me.

I'd like to thank my spiritual confidante, Jacques McNeil for all her prayers and support. My friends who have supported me over the years Donna Broussard, Veronica Benion, Carolyn & John Denham, Lois & Larry Gamell, Denise & Tyrone Hampton, Janet Heard, and Felicia Jones.

I thank my cousin Glen for sharing this historical time period of his life with me. I thank my cousin Dwayne for all of his inspiring words.

Most of all, I thank my mom for loving me and never accepting less than the best from me. I thank my Marty Daddy for being my daddy; I love the both of you.

Table of Contents

This book is dedicated to my son Jaydon,....... the love of my life and in memory of Trayvon Martin and Kendrec McDade; two young black men who lost their lives in the battle of senseless social injustices.

Prologue

For the first 4 ½ years of my little life, there was only me and mommy. We lived off and on with her mom, Grandma Roses, and Grandpa Mac, her step dad. At that age, all I wanted to do was become an acrobatic gymnast, after I had seen them on television flipping and flying around at Grandma's house. Aunt Julia and Uncles Ken, Stanley, and Wesley lived there too; they are her youngest siblings, not much older than I, and boy, did we have a huge family! My mom had six sisters and four brothers: with her included, eleven children in all. There are 41 first cousins, and I'm the eleventh. My mom and her sisters were tight; they were best friends. Aunts Thelma and Francis, are the two oldest sisters, and Allen, the oldest brother, was everyone's favorite; we called him Uncle Bud.

In the mornings, before work, Uncle Bud or one of my aunts would stop by Grandma's house to indulge in a breakfast of eggs, toast, bacon with rinds and a cup of freshly perked, Hills Brothers coffee. And on the weekends everyone would meet at Grandma's house for Sunday dinner. My mom and aunties would sit around the kitchen table drinking coffee, sharing stories, gossiping, and cackling into hysteria while preparing a family feast. My cousins and I were attached like siblings. We would play "Tag", "Green Light Go," "Simon Says," and "Hide-and–Go-Seek." After dinner, sad at being forced to part, we'd all begin to cry because we didn't want to leave one another. We'd literally boo-hoo as though we weren't going to see each other ever again, as each sister rounded up her children en route to the exit from the backyard.

Together, the seven sisters birthed three to four children every other year. Between 1963 and 1965, seven of us came into the world: me to my mom Helen, Dwayne and Morgan to Aunt Tootie, Troy and Sherry to Aunt Bruce, Gailyn and Glen (aka Rodney G. King) to Aunt Dessa. The seven of us were thick as thieves growing up. All of us were born and raised in Northern California, but Aunt Dessa's family moved to Southern California.

My mom and I moved to Pasadena and stayed for a while with my Aunt Dessa and Uncle Ronnie, her husband. I remember having so much fun with my two little boy cousins: Gailyn and Glen. Uncle Ronnie would take us to the park during the day when my mom was working at the local convalescent home. We would "log roll" through the grass at the park, swing, and slide, all day long. Sometimes in the evening, we'd go to Uncle Ronnie's mom's house. They called her Grandma Libby. A couch swing hung from the huge avocado tree in her back yard; Gailyn, Glen, and I would pick and eat the avocadoes while swinging leisurely, until the adults would call us for dinner. It wasn't long before my grandma summoned us back to Sacramento; so there we were, back on the Greyhound bus, stopping at every imaginable depot from LA to Sacramento.

In fact, the Greyhound bus depot in Sacramento is where my mom met my step–dad, a professional, heavyweight boxer out of Canton, Ohio. Within a year, they got married, much to my own elation! I called him my Marty-Daddy. We moved in San Francisco, a huge city in comparison to Sacramento. Initially, we lived in the

Hayes Valley district in an apartment complex that was also home to a few of dad's boxer friends.

Lots of things were happening: my Marty-Daddy constantly trained for fights, and often he'd take me to the gym with him. He sparred with Sonny Liston when he'd come to town; he knew Joe Frazier and George Foreman. A rising star, he was training for the upcoming championship fight. Before that fight, he had one more hurdle to clear, a bout with a guy named Manuel Ramos. The bout was in Texas. During the fight, however, he suffered a serious injury – a detached retina that ended his career. When he came back to California, I remember Uncle Ronnie's sister Ann being really pissed off and cursing him like a sailor about losing her $500.00 on that fight.

Before we knew it we were living in the Potrero Hills Projects, where athletes like OJ Simpson were raised. The people of the projects were so sad; the despair in their eyes was visible. I would hear Ms. Reed telling Mommy that families lived there for generations, and one day she and her kids were getting out. The day Dr. Martin Luther King died, the entire community cried and sobbed. They threw their arms up in frustration, wailing and exclaiming, "Who do we have now? What hope is there for us now?"

It was a time when we kids latched arms together in a straight line as we skipped down the steep hill of Missouri Street in unison, shouting, "Say it loud! I'm black and I'm proud!" It was not until later in life that I truly understood how important these lyrics were to our community. Most of the kids were hungry, poor, deprived, and neglected; but there I was too, marching for the cause, right along with them. Although I was only about five or six at the time, I still remember the sense of sadness and hopelessness lurking in the air back then – a feeling that mingled with the stench of dog poop and garbage, mixed with a hint of wild licorice plants and Eucalyptus trees, which covered the hilly fields surrounding the apartments.

The people had had enough of discrimination and poverty. Angela Davis, Hughey Newton, and Eldridge Clever were on the scene back then, fighting against the system! You heard poor black people talking about a revolution! "And let's get rid of Nixon!" is what they were saying. I didn't know what that meant, nor did I imagine that one day, much later, I'd be right back in the middle of a similar scene.

By then, my mom and all her siblings, with the exception of two, were Jehovah's Witnesses. As Witnesses, we accepted the concept that our family and the congregation members were our only friends and family. This Christian denomination seemed to have sealed our family bond even tighter because it excluded the association with worldly people - in other words, anyone who was not a Witness.

Every year we'd have a huge assembly at the Dodger Stadium or the Oakland Coliseum. When the assembly was in Oakland, all of the family members would stay in our three-bedroom project apartment. We kids loved it! We'd have so much fun playing and talking all through the night when we were supposed to be asleep.

Almost every year, Aunt Dessa and Uncle Ronnie would drive up to visit everyone. Because I was Uncle Ronnie's favorite niece, their first stop was San Francisco. They didn't have any girls yet. Gailyn, Glen, and I would play like crazy for a few days – sitting on the stairs and rolling down to the bottom like little cars rolling over bumps. Uncle Ronnie would then talk mom into letting me drive to Sacramento with them. He'd say, "Oh, come on Sis! I'ma pick up the other kids in Sacramento, and I'm taking everybody fishing at the American River." I was his girl! Actually, the only kids going fishing with him were Gailyn, Glen, and myself.

Eventually, I had my own little brothers and sister: Douglas, Juline, and Earl. Mommy had trained me to be a surrogate mom to them. I loved them to death, but boy was I tired of feeding, changing, dressing, and cleaning up after them. That became my routine until I left home. We moved from the projects not long after my baby brother, Douglas, was born; and once my little sister, Juline, was born, we bought our first, brand new house in Pittsburg, California – a city in Contra Costa County. My parents eventually left the Jehovah's Witness faith, which allowed me to pursue my childhood dream of becoming a gymnast. Although I started later than others, I excelled in competitions and rose to the state's number one rank in my class in the NCS Gymnastic Champion ranking number.

Another of my childhood dreams was to work at NASA in Cocoa Beach, Florida, like Major Tony Nelson from "I Dream of Jeannie." Well, I never made it to Cocoa Beach or became an astronaut; but I did work at Jet Propulsion Laboratory/NASA in Pasadena, California for over a decade. It turned out to be more of a nightmare than a dream.

A Letter to my Cousin -
Unadulterated and Unapologetic

Glen,

I want you to know how I feel, but every time I try to tell you, a lump rises in my throat and I can't get it all out. You usually shrug your shoulders, and say, "Cous, you know I didn't say those things," and walk away. That hurts even more because you're running from me. I never ran from you. You know you're my boy and all, and we fought some damn good fights together, but the one between us was gut-wrenching, ugly and demoralizing for me, and you need to understand that, and embrace it. There was no rhyme or reason to it.

I poured all of my heart and strength into protecting you from the venomous hatred spewed out from communities when you disappointed them, time and time again. I tried to help you manage your stress, and made sure you had adequate legal representation for the aftermath when you couldn't. I stood up for you when no one else, genuinely, would. You need to understand the passion and effort I poured into promoting your dream of having a record label, and materializing it for you because I believed in you. It was for the love of family that made me make sure you saw your kids every week; and they were provided with everything you had. When all was said and done, I just wanted the best for you. I wanted you and our family to go down in history in a way that would've made Grandma Roses really proud.

I don't understand how all of that translated into me being "Triece – the bad guy." I never thought in a million years you'd turn on me like that. What did I ever do to you? I keep asking myself that question, over and over again. Even now, when you come to my house, and we're talking….when I look into your eyes, you drop your head or turn away. I know you feel me asking you that same question, without speaking one word. I'm having a hard time right now even composing this letter to you because I still can't get it out without crying. It is easier for me to believe that you didn't say those awful things about me, and that maybe you just didn't defend me when they were being said. Either way, I don't know which is the lesser of the two evils, in my mind.

I can get past the loss of money and credit – that's the risk of business investments. Nobody wants to take a hit, but they do everyday. At my lowest moment, when my credit was gone to shit, no one would rent to me. They didn't even want my money because of the water damage to the rental property you allowed your ex-wife to destroy that was under my name. But still, I could live with that. The difficult part was when I called our family members up north to get help, and no one would help me. Everybody, including my own siblings, wanted to know what I did with your money. If it weren't for Carolyn and John letting me rent a room from them, I would have been in a homeless shelter or out in the streets; but that didn't seem to faze you or anyone else in the family. They weren't even part of our family – just good people we met and hired to work on the music project. I couldn't even get a telephone for my room because your friend ran up the telephone bill that was in my name. And for what? But, just when I thought I had seen it all, I was served with a lawsuit where you let another female friend of yours run into someone's vehicle while driving the truck you asked me to put in my name for your convenience. Aunt Dessa accused me of getting credit cards under your name. And guess what? I was hurt and anguished, but I found a way to swallow the humiliation and live with it too. But what I haven't been able to live with – the most difficult part for me to digest – was when one of your female friends said Ann told her, 'I was sleeping with you, and everyone in the family knew that's how I stole all your money, and that's why I didn't want her to be with you'. I've never felt that level of demoralization in my entire life. I mean, incest? Really? Who does that? You let your friends and our family members attack and degrade my character, when I spent years protecting yours. So my next question to you is, did it take away your pain to join in and watch pain inflicted on me?

The only way I've been able to make sense of all of this is that the pain inflicted on you through the beating, the loss of your case against the attorneys, and the friends that betrayed you was too much. When you needed to lash out, I just happened to be there. Honestly, I don't really know what to think. But what I do know is that I feel betrayed; and I know when you come over and spend time with my Jaydon, that is your way of apologizing. When you make the comment, "Cous, you deserve a lot more in life than what he had to offer," it's your way of complimenting me. But for whatever reason, it's not enough, I need a better explanation.

Love you always and family forever,
Ontresicia

Chapter One
March 3, 1991

I t was March 3, 1991 when I received a call from Auntie Dessa. "Treesa," she said, using my nickname from her and most of the family, "Auntie needs some help. Glen was in an accident last night with the police." She was talking about her son, my cousin Rodney King, who we all call Glen.

"What kind of accident?" I asked. I also was a little stunned because I didn't know he had been released from prison yet.

"I don't know, I got a call this morning and I had to go down to the county jail. They acted like they didn't want me to see him, but when I got in….my baby was laying there with his body covered all the way up to his head. Treesa, Glen's head and face were so swollen, I could hardly recognize him; he didn't look like himself." Her voice trembled as she paused, seemingly to hold back from crying. "Anyway, the police said I'ma need a criminal defense attorney. Some friends and I have made some calls, and it turns out, all of these attorneys want at least $5,000 before they'll get started. I'm trying to raise the money. Do you have any money?"

"Well. I have my tuition money; but don't worry, I'll call Aunt Tootie and Aunt Lootie to see if I can raise the money for you." Aunt Dessa was a devout Witness, even after most of our family had turned away from the religion. Aunt Dessa wasn't close with many members of the family since they were no longer part of the faith. Although I wasn't practicing the faith either, for some reason I remained in Aunt Dessa's good graces. I was her link to the rest of the family. Aunt Lootie, however, was still a Witness, but when I called her and explained what had happened to Glen, she blurted, "I don't have no money." I asked Aunt Lootie to tell Uncle Bud to call me, but he never did. Since Glen had just recently been released from prison, maybe that's why the family wasn't too quick to give up their hard-earned cash. It was late that Sunday afternoon. I had just come in from the grocery store when I got the call. After talking to my Aunt Dessa, I jumped into motion with phone calls. I expected I'd have a much better chance of getting in touch with people since it was the weekend. As I put away my food, I had the phone to my ear, talking to each family member.

My cousin Debra, Aunt Tootie's daughter, said she'd give me $250, and I had my $250 tuition money. That was all I was able to raise, $500 out of the $5000 Aunt Dessa needed. I called my friends Tyrone Hampton, who was the president of the Pasadena/Altadena Black Business Association (BBA), and his wife Denise Hampton, to see if they could give me a referral for an attorney. I explained to them what little I knew about Glen being beaten and that I needed to find a good attorney who would help us and work with us for the retainer fees.

Tyrone gave me the number for Skip Cooper, president of the LA Chapter BBA, and good friends with Johnnie Cochran. He told me to tell Skip that he had referred me. Based on the story I told Tyrone, he felt I needed to get in touch with Johnnie Cochran.

While folding the grocery bags, I paused for a few seconds to grab the pen and write down the number. Then, I called Skip immediately and told him everything. He said Johnnie was in Georgia on business, but to call his office and leave a message with his staff that Skip had referred me.

Monday morning, March 4, I swerved into the cold damp parking structure of the Jet Propulsion Lab (JPL) Foothill building, slung my badge against the ID reader, and pulled into a parking space on the first floor. My stomach was in knots every time I entered the building, and today was worse. Not only did I have to deal with the everyday stresses this placed caused me, but now I had to prepare for another fight. Although I didn't have a lot of details as to what had occurred when Glen was arrested, I knew two things: he was beaten pretty badly, and the police were responsible.

Around this time, a few of us African-Americans were in the middle of an investigation at JPL for the disparity of treatment against blacks in the company. Still, going through the investigations from the complaints we had filed with the Employee Relations department months ago, we were all nervous about what would happen to us. Yet, we stood our ground. The only black manager at JPL at the time was a man I'll call Roger, the Contractor's Capability Manager who had been at JPL for a long time. He was a tall, big-boned man – not really fat, but not muscular either, and just over six feet tall. He had a caramel tone with sideburns that curved into his full beard. He had very thin lips for a black man and spoke with an educated southern accent. Most of us blacks at the company were oblivious to what was going on. We knew as individuals we were not being treated fairly, but since we didn't talk about it, in fear of retaliation or being labeled as a troublemaker, we kept our thoughts to ourselves. It was Roger who brought us together in a private

11

meeting to point out the disparities between us and our white counterparts.

After several meetings, and comparing notes, we decided together to file a complaint to the Employee Relations department in mid-summer of 1990. In general, we had common experiences. We noticed that most of us were not being promoted within the same time period as our white peers. We also realized there was a gross pay inequity between us and our white peers. It was said that we "didn't have enough education to be promoted and we needed higher degrees". But we had witnessed our peers of other races being promoted in the past without degrees. They had been promoted on experience and years served with the company. By the time we could show years served and experience, the rules had conveniently changed. So we worked twice as hard to obtain a degree so there would be no logical reason for another denial. Then they came up with other excuses like, we "had writing deficiencies" or we "were difficult to get along with"; so for the past nine months, we'd been walking on egg shells awaiting the outcome of our investigation.

I was anxious to get to my desk so that I could begin making more calls to help Aunt Dessa find a lawyer – preferably Johnnie Cochran. As I rushed through the door toward the entrance to the building, I waved and shouted for the two ladies that worked on the same floor as me to hold the elevator. But wouldn't you know it, they didn't. I guess they didn't hear or see me, but this was of no surprise to me. Some of the staff there made it publicly known their dislike towards me and some of the other blacks – especially after complaints had been filed.

I finally made it to my desk and started making calls before I could get too busy with work. I spoke with someone from Johnnie's office, and though his name eludes my memory, I will never forget the conversation. After I told him the story of my cousin being beaten by the police, he said, "Really, Miss? Black men are beat down and killed by the police every day, and you say your cousin had a record? No one really cares much about situations like this. These incidents happen all the time. Can you tell me why the police beat him?"

I slouched back in my chair and mumbled, "No. I don't know."

"Give me your number, I'll tell Johnnie you called when he returns," he replied.

His words, "No one really cares….this happens all the time" reminded me of my own issues with JPL. As my day went on, I snuck in calls to other lawyers, but it was like the man at Johnnie's office said: no one really cared.

Early in 1982, my Aunt Dessa witnessed me struggling to work two jobs – two dead-end jobs. She told me I should apply at JPL. She said, "You're so smart, you could probably get a job there".

I said, "What's JPL?"

"It's NASA," she said.

I remembered my childhood dream and immediately did my research to find out what I needed to do to apply at JPL. After researching, applying and passing a couple of tests, Aunt Dessa was driving me to my interview at JPL. I got the job and began working on April 6, 1982.

So okay, maybe I wasn't an astronaut, but I was sure as hell at NASA! I was a naïve eighteen-year-old, and really had long forgotten my dreams of working at NASA in Coco Beach Florida, like Tony from "I Dream of Jeannie." But it all came back to me as I entered the Visitors Control Center at 4800 Oak Grove Drive. I was welcomed by a pretty, caramel-skinned, black lady in a dark suit – very professional, and with a look of distinguished pride on her face. Her name was Bobby. She gave me instructions on what I needed to do and where I needed to go to obtain my security badge. I tried to pay attention to her, but my eyes were drawn to the federal emblem on the floor and the round NASA/JPL emblem on the wall behind her. It was then the butterflies awakened in my stomach. Everything I had ever imagined or dreamed of as a child was about to come true. This was the beginning of my journey to my career. I was proud just to be there. I was hired with the job title of Buyers Aid; however, on the first day of work, I was sent to fill in for an Administrative Aid, a black lady named Tiffany, who was out on maternity leave.

A Buyers Aid executed small dollar procurement acquisitions up to $2,500. When Tiffany returned, I continued to work as an Administrative Aid. Although I was still new to the company, I wanted to work as a Buyers Aid as I was hired to do and as everyone that shared the same title was given the opportunity to do. When I spoke to my supervisor, he said, "It should be a privilege for you to be working at the Jet Propulsion Lab." I was told I wouldn't be able to start buying until I received my two-year degree. However, at that time, a two-year degree plus two years' experience with a good evaluation meant you qualified for a Buyer I position. This was the beginning of my nightmare.

Back then, most, if not all, of the business processes were handled manually. For instance, one purchase order was twelve sheets of paper separated by carbon sheets and bonded together. The last four copies were of no use to anyone – just extras. Most of the time, the secretary would staple the extra sheets to the back of the fifth copy and mail to the requestor. This was normal practice. Although the description of the request was typed out and legible on all copies, the handwritten area such as your signature and buyer code was not legible on the last four copies of the purchase order. Later I found out that my immediate supervisor, a man I'll call Chris and who despised me, used this company practice to begin building a case against me and to discredit my reputation of having an excellent work ethic.

A couple of years later, after graduating from community college in Pasadena in 1984, I was promoted to a first level Senior Buyer Aid position at JPL. The pay increase was smaller than I had hoped for, and I could hardly pay rent, eat, or clothe myself. But everyone I knew would always say, "You work for a blue chip company."…. "It's NASA. It will never go out of business, so don't worry about the money you'll get it eventually, and you'll be able to retire there."…."You know most black people can't get into companies like that." By now, there were other concerns besides pay; like discrimination and harassment that went on at JPL. I expressed this to some colleagues and friends, but their reaction basically told me that no one really cared…it happened all the time. I was just "lucky" to be at such a prestigious company, so I kept my mouth shut – at least for a while. Little did I know, my experiences that everyone claimed were "normal" would turn out to be the onset of even greater injustices, injustices that would come to a head in Corporate America at the same time when the African-American community suddenly stood up and said, "No, it's not okay anymore!"

I informed my aunt of my unsuccessful attempts to attain Glen a lawyer who would work with us on the retainer fees. "I'll try again tomorrow, Aunt Dessa."

Chapter Two
Caught On Tape

The next day, Aunt Dessa called me. "Treesa, the KTLA News people called me and told me I need to go to the station to see a videotape that a man named George Holiday had submitted to them showing Glen being beaten by those cops." She said, "They said they would play this tape on the five o'clock news today, so I needed to go to the station to preview the tape because it was quite graphic."

"OK. Do you have anyone to go with you? Is Holly there?"

"Yes. She's going with me."

"OK. I'll come by after I get off of work."

Later, I found out while Aunt Dessa was still there, someone at the station slipped her the number for an attorney named Robert Rentzer. After viewing the tape, I can only imagine how distraught she was. Maybe that's why she hired Robert Rentzer immediately.

After I got off of work, I hurried to the parking lot, jumped in my shiny brown metallic Volkswagen bug, and jetted out the parking structure for Altadena Dr., and then on to the 210 freeway. Aunt Dessa didn't live too far from where I worked so I was at her house within ten minutes. She lived on a small street off Orange Grove lined with big beautiful trees. I remember being at her house on hot summer days sitting in front of the house shaded by the huge trees.

As I approached the house, I noticed a couple of cars already parked on the worn-down asphalt disguised as a driveway.

The house was small but with a nice-sized porch that supported a small two-seater and matching chair wicker set. Inside were my aunt's friend, Holly, who lived with her, Aunt Dessa's daughter, my cousin, Tasha, and another lady, that I had never seen, awaiting the big news break. The living room was the first room you entered. The couch was against the back wall facing the front door and a chair sat to the left of the couch. The floor model television was in the right corner of the small room. Down a short hallway, past the dining room, was the kitchen towards the back of the house. That's where I noticed Aunt Dessa scurrying around when I entered. While speaking to my cousin and the other ladies, I waved to my Aunt Dessa, acknowledging that I had heard her calling me when I first entered.

After swapping pleasantries, I finally made it to Aunt Dessa, gave her a big hug, and asked if she was OK and if she needed my help with anything? She nodded while saying "Yeah baby, Auntie is okay." It was just minutes before five, so everyone began gathering around the television. I was surprised that my uncle Wesley wasn't there, but then again, none of us yet understood the enormity of this tape or Glen's brush with the law this time.

As soon as the news came on, the big story was the "videotape of the beating of Rodney King by four white policemen." To the world, it was just some random black man, but for my family, he was a cousin, son, grandson, and nephew. We sat and looked on in horror as we saw a member of our family being brutally beaten by the police. I stood in the back in the hallway, glancing at the video a few times while going back and forth to the kitchen to finish with the food Aunt Dessa was preparing, so that I wouldn't study it as the others did. I saw bits and pieces, but never watched the entire video and tried not to listen.

I felt I had been and was still being beaten down and stripped of my dignity in Corporate America; and now I was watching my family being beaten down in the street like a modern-day slave. I went toward the back and leaned against the wall. I tried to take in a deep breath but could only manage short breaths. Fearing I was about to start hyper–ventilating, I closed my eyes to slow my breathing down. A warm tingling feeling ran through my body. All I could do was say to myself, "Not now." This was not the time to let it all out. This was a time for me to pull up whatever I had left inside of me and prepare for another fight against injustice. Working at JPL, I had been subjected to a society that accepted and planned institutionalized racism, but I'd be damned if I would stand idly by and watch my cousin be stripped away of his human rights by this society while being told it's his fault.

I pulled myself together once again and kept my emotions intact. I had become this stoic, ultra-conservative person as a result from the injustices and discrimination I faced daily while working in Corporate America. I had trained myself to show no feelings or emotions when things went badly, even when they were really bad. Besides, someone needed to remain calm through all of this, why not me – I was used to it. I had become good at it. But, I wondered during this time if I had become calm and professional or had simply become desensitized to the black community's plight? There had been many incidents of injustice in the black community that affected me, but perhaps not the way it should have. Had I become whitewashed by

Corporate America? I have to admit that before Glen had been beaten by the police, I had heard of many instances in which police were accused of excessive force, but I had bought into that myth that we all had the same opportunities. If I could do it – get into college and find a good job – everyone else in the community could do the same.

Most of my young adult life, I was consumed and self-absorbed with my own woes. I couldn't feel the pain of our people or any other people who I perceived as not contributing to society. I thought, *Damned the plight and struggle of a black man. What about me? What about all the other black women who graduated from college to enter the workforce only to be humiliated, annihilated of her dignity, and stripped of her very being, just to barely earn enough money to buy a bus pass, pay rent, feed and cloth, and comfort her babies abandoned by the black man – the same man who decided to cuss out the white employer and quit, or get fired from the job all in the same day or week after starting? If I had to be subjected to this insanity, why shouldn't everyone else endure? Besides, what gave them the right to give up like that when I couldn't?*

That's how I felt until then, but this event would change my thinking about everything I had experienced in life up to that point. I saw and felt his pain as my own painful experience at JPL, but what made Glen's experience worse was that his attackers knew nothing of him nor had they ever seen him before. Yet, they almost killed him, just because he fit into their stereotypical profile. The deep, wide wound inflicted on me by the tragedy and trauma of what happened to Glen allowed me to feel the pain of our people and others alike. I was already weak, broken, and tired from fighting my own battle but the savage assault on my cousin provoked enough anger to empower me and revive my strength to fight harder. So I did.

The day after publicly showing my cousin being beaten like a wild animal on the streets – no, I take that back, they wouldn't even beat a wild animal the way Glen had been attacked – my home and work phones were flooded with calls from all sorts of lawyers wanting to help us. I don't know how some of these people got my number. I had made a few calls, but not that many. There were even calls from some of the same lawyers I had called the day before. Now I guess they saw the dollar signs flashing before their eyes. Before the tape aired, no one would take the case on a contingent assignment. With the tape, however, they were sure to get millions and their cut would be hefty. The lawyers were ready to cash in on Glen's injustice.

Johnnie Cochran was the first call I received. Unfortunately, it was too late to hire him at that time because Aunt Dessa had already hired Robert Rentzer. This had already become a very political incident. Here was this white attorney about to represent a black man who had been beaten by three white policemen and one Hispanic officer. I guess Robert Rentzer knew this was over his head, so he quickly hired Steve Lerman to work with him.

"Hello Ms. Averette. This is Johnnie Cochran returning your call. I saw what happened to your brother."

"I didn't think you were interested in the case." I said.

"No it's not that. I was finishing up on another case where a para-plegic was found hung in his jail cell. As you can probably imagine I had to stay focused and finalize that case before jumping into another."

"Oh, I definitely understand. Well my aunt, Glen's mother, al-ready hired a lawyer. By the way, we call Rodney by his middle name, Glen, and he's my cousin, not my brother. Anyway, she hired an attorney named Robert Rentzer. Do you know him?" Before he could answer I blurted out, "Someone from the station gave her his card when she was there yesterday."

"What?" He became very agitated with this information. He told me this was against some kind of regulation or policy. No one should have been referring any lawyers to my aunt. He asked me to tell him who had done this. The tone and excitement of his voice made it clear this was a big issue. He asked me if the person worked at the station or was it just some passerby or what, but I had no answers for him. In concluding my interrogation, he said, "If you need anything, feel free to call me and keep me posted because I'm very interested in this case. This kind of thing sickens me."

I thought it was very nice of Johnnie to tell me to keep him posted because he's a very brilliant and sought-after lawyer. He gave me his personal number. I was impressed and I could feel he was genuine. As the day went on, I spoke to many lawyers but none of the other lawyers told me to call if I needed anything. Once they heard another lawyer had already been hired, good-bye and *click* was all I heard.

Meanwhile, it had been really tense at work since we filed that complaint. As a Senior Buyer Aid, I probably executed about twenty-five to thirty-five procurement acquisitions per day. It seemed I had to always be on guard at work. No matter how hard I worked, my supervisor seemed to constantly look for ways to discredit me.

❧

I had returned to work after being sick for a couple of days. I went to my desk and noticed my files were missing from my desk. I went to my immediate supervisor, Chris, to inquire about the whereabouts of my files.

"I have them. I'm auditing all of your files."

"Auditing? Why?" I asked.

"Don't you worry about it. You'll be well informed by the time I'm finished." We were always at odds, especially after I had spoken to his manager, who I'll call Mr. Cotter, the Section Manager, about my chances of being promoted to a Buyer I position after my graduation. Mr. Cotter was in his mid-sixties and had a round pudgy tummy, with gray hair, blue eyes, and chubby sagging cheeks. Mr. Cotter thought I had great work ethics and Chris hated that his manager had given me a compliment. When he finished with his audit, he called me into his office. I was surprised to see Mr. Cotter sitting in the office as well. I was so nervous. I couldn't have imagined what he found to warrant immediate termination. I thought that would be the only reason to pull Mr. Cotter into this.

"As you know Ontresicia, I have been auditing your files," he said in a professional manner, but I could feel the venom shooting from his eyes.

"Yes," I answered.

"Well, I've found that none of your purchase orders had a legible signature on all copies, nor could I see the buyer code on all sheets."

I sat there dumbfounded, wondering what to do. "I don't understand; can I see them?" I managed to ask.

"Sure. " He turned to the right of his desk and pulled out a huge folder. He sifted through a few papers and handed me one of my purchase orders. I flipped through the pages quickly and noticed the only copies where my signature was not legible were the last four copies.

"My signature is legible on all copies except for the last four copies." I looked at him, baffled as to why I was in his office and why Mr. Cotter had been included in this meeting.

"Let me see that Ontresicia," Mr. Cotter demanded. After sifting through the pages, he looked at Chris and asked, "Why are you so concerned with copies no one really uses? Is there something I'm missing?"

To save face, he answered, "Well, Mr. Cotter, all copies should be legible regardless of what we use them for." I raised my brow as if to say, *Since when?* But I remained quiet and allowed him to continue digging his own grave. Mr. Cotter didn't say another word, but just got up and walked out of the office. I wanted to jump up and stick my tongue out and say, "Na na na na na, now you're sitting here looking like Boo Boo the fool," but I remained cool. I didn't expect an apology, nor did I expect the next words that came from his mouth. As he watched to make sure Mr. Cotter was out of hearing range of the office he got up and closed the door.

"You over-confident little….." I guess he came to some senses and decided not to allow that last thought to come out of his mouth. "You obviously have Mr. Cotter in your corner for whatever reason but my advice to you is that you better think twice before going over my head soliciting yourself for any position here again. I am the one who will decide when or if you ever get a buyer position. Is that clear?"

"Yes." That day, the lights came on. He was upset because I had spoken to his manager about a future promotion after receiving my Bachelor's degree. He thought I had too much confidence in myself. *How dare I not be satisfied with just being here? How dare I have the audacity to want more?*

∾

I could barely wait to get off work so I could get into my car, turn the radio to "the Wave", and let some smooth jazz take my thoughts away. One of my favorite songs from Alex Bugnon was just ending, and then I heard the radio DJs talking about Glen. I listened to them talk for a couple of minutes but decided to turn the station to some R & B, but all the stations were consumed with discussion and dialogue about Glen. Listeners were calling in and the common thread of all the calls was, "I'm glad we got it on tape." Many people, not just blacks, felt this happened often but no one could prove it. It was the police's word against them. Now, we had proof. Most of the callers spoke as if this was their fight, not just Glen's. They spoke as "we" and "us." It was a new camaraderie.

Back in Sacramento, where most of our family resided, the incident threw most of my aunts, uncles, and cousins into an emotional scurry. The family had been very distant from one another for years. Since we had such a large family, it was common for one sister to be angry at another because a nephew or niece had disrespected an elder or had been living a lifestyle opposed to the strict upbringing set by Grandma Roses and reinforced by the Jehovah's Witness religion we had all been raised in or born into.

My mom and her sisters would disagree about things like what a certain scripture in the Bible really meant, or the correct way to serve Jehovah. Well, I guess it's true what some say, "A tragedy will tear a family apart or bring them closer." Thankfully, that was the one good thing that came from this catastrophe – at least at the beginning. It definitely brought us closer than we had been in years – before the split in our beliefs. The siblings cried together while they prepared food to take to the capitol building during the protest they staged in Sacramento. My mom, her sisters, Bruce and Bernice, and her brother Stanley all were interviewed in the Northern California area. They were all very vocal about their feelings that this was a racially motivated incident.

A couple of days later, I went to visit my aunt to make sure she was okay and to see what was going on with Glen. I pulled into the driveway and trotted up the steps to the door. I knocked several times. It was dark, so I wondered if anyone was home. Then the door inched slowly open. There were no lights on but I could see the glow from the television. "Aunt Dessa?"

"Oh, is that you Treesa?" She answered in a raspy voice.

"Yes. Why aren't the lights on?" She opened the door suspiciously to let me in.

"That lawyer said he was getting threats about Glen."

"Threats?" I said. I thought maybe Aunt Dessa misunderstood whatever Lerman had told her. Seeing her son beaten and having to deal with lawyers was probably making her a little paranoid. "Auntie, I'm sure it'll be okay to turn on some lights." She watched me as I flipped the light switch. Then I took her hand and escorted her to the couch where we sat. "Aunt Dessa, how are you doing? You're not scared, are you?"

"I just don't know what's going on," she said, shaking her head.

"Well look, I wanted to talk to you about something. You know this case is getting a lot of attention because the beating was caught on tape. Some of the local African-American leaders advised me that Johnnie Cochran should be representing Glen. He's the best person for this job. Johnnie called me a couple of days ago and expressed an interest in the case." Before I could finish she had started shaking her head. "Aunt Dessa, you can't get any better than Johnnie Cochran. He's like one of the biggest attorneys in the country." I asked doubt-fully, "Would you consider releasing Robert Rentzer and Steve Lermam?"

"No," she snapped. "Jehovah sent him to me so we don't need another attorney." After that comment, I left it alone. I knew she wouldn't budge on her decision since she believed Jehovah had sent him. I asked her about Glen; she told me he was out of the hospital and Lerman had him staying somewhere away from the public, but he was okay.

When I returned home that evening, I had a message from Ty-rone Hampton asking me to call him regarding Glen. I decided to take care of whatever business I needed to attend to before taking a much-needed hot bath. I placed my books on the table and even before taking off my shoes, sat down to call Tyrone.

"Hello, it's Ontresicia, how are you? I just got in and heard your message, what's up?"

"Hey Ontresicia, how was your day?"

"It was okay. Pretty busy since that tape aired. I've been receiving a lot of calls from lawyers. Johnnie called earlier this week also."

"Well, that's the reason I called. I've been talking to a few people – very influential people in the community – and they are all telling me to get the message to you or your family that you definitely need Johnnie Cochran for this case."

"Yes, I agree but unfortunately, this is out of my hands. I already told my Aunt Dessa that he was interested in the case. I'm sure you know by now she has hired that Robert Rentzer lawyer and he added Steve Lerman to be lead counsel. That's been on the news too. She told me she wouldn't release him."

"That's another thing I wanted to talk to you about. A very reliable friend of mine told me that he had first-hand knowledge that Rentzer had been disbarred before and neither he nor Lerman had ever worked a case of this magnitude before. Johnnie is the only lawyer for this community that can handle such a high profile case."

"I understand. Well, the only thing I can do is talk to Aunt Dessa again. But I appreciate you calling to inform me. Thank you."

"OK. Ontresicia you know you can call me anytime if you need anything. I'll talk to you later. Bye"

After hanging up, my mind needed a break. I turned on the water and poured my lavender and chamomile bubble bath into the tub. While the water for my bath was running I went back into the living room, selected my favorite Billie Holiday CD, poured myself a glass of wine, and hurried back to the bath. I lit the candles that surrounded the tub, turned off all of the lights, and submerged myself. I took a sip of wine, placed the glass back on the edge of the tub and closed my eyes. I tried not to think about the conversation I had just had with Tyrone, but the promise I made to myself to do everything I could so that Glen would not have to suffer the humiliation of being demeaned or degraded without recourse weighed heavily on my mind. Tyrone and Skip were the local black community leaders and most of his circle of friends were activists – people in high positions. I looked up to and admired Tyrone and his wife. I wanted to do the right thing and the smart thing by my cousin, but on the issue of which lawyer would represent him, there was really nothing I could do.

That Saturday morning, I got up and planned to visit Glen and get some chores done. As I stripped my bed and carried the sheets to the hamper, the phone rang. I dropped the sheets on the floor and dashed for the phone.

"Hello Ontresicia, it's Johnnie," spoke the voice on the other end. "I am calling to let you know you need to get a message to Lerman. More than three days has passed and he hasn't taken any pictures of Rodney yet. It is very important to get pictures taken before the swelling and bruises began to dissipate." He spoke fast and I tried to catch every detail of our conversation.

"OK. I will get the message to him immediately."

"How are you and the family doing?"

"Oh, we're okay. Thank you."

"OK, well get that message to Lerman right away."

"I will. Thanks again for calling. Bye." In a short time frame and just from the second time speaking with Johnnie, I felt the urgency to do what he said and when he said to do it. He just had that effect on me.

I knew Glen had left the hospital and was in some private location, so I called Aunt Dessa to see where he was. I hadn't thought about it before, but after that conversation with Johnnie, I was reminded that Glen was in bad shape, so why would he be in some private location without his family? He was too hurt to take care of himself. "Hi Aunt Dessa, how are you doing today?"

"I'm okay. How are you?"

"I'm good. I was thinking about visiting Glen today, can you give me his information?"

She paused for a few seconds before snapping, "Lerman will give you Glen's information when he feels it's OK for you to have it."

29

"I don't understand. I wouldn't do anything to cause harm to Glen. I won't give the information to anyone else."

"Like I said, Lerman will give the information when he's ready for you to have it."

"OK. I'll talk to you later." I was a tad pissed off to say the least. It seems she didn't have any problem giving me information when she needed my help. I also believed she feared I would be able to convince Glen to release Lerman and hire Johnnie, therefore, not really wanting me to speak with Glen.

The next day, still boiling, I decided to call Aunt Dessa again but she wasn't home. Glen's younger sister Tasha answered the phone. I spoke with her and she told me no one in the family was to have Glen's information, but she gave me the phone number and password anyway. He was in some hotel under a different name – in a safe place.

I quickly punched the numbers in the phone and gave the password to the hotel employee. "Hey Glen, how are you?"

"I'm okay," he mumbled.

He didn't sound okay, but I continued with the business at hand. "You know Johnnie Cochran is interested in representing you."

"Mom already hired someone."

"I know but –"

"I don't want Mommy to get sick again," he snapped.

I jumped and took a quick glance at the phone. I had hit an unexpected nerve. "Sick? What happened?"

"She lost her fuckin' mind last night. Something like a breakdown or something...they had to take her to the hospital last night. This is too much for her. I don't want to stress her out any more."

"OK. I understand. Don't worry, I'll try to help look out for her. I need Steve's number so I can give him a message from Johnnie. So are you doing okay?"

Back to being barely audible, he said. "I'ma be alright."

"Why are you in a hotel under a different name? Are you getting threats or something? What's going on?"

"Steve thought it would be better if I stayed low key for a while. He doesn't really want me talking to anyone."

"But why didn't he tell us? We're not just anyone; we're your family." Before he could answer, I thought, *why am I stressing him out?* "Well, I guess he did tell Tasha and Aunt Dessa so I guess he thought they'd let the rest of us know, upon their discretion. Anyway, call me if you need anything. I'll let you rest now." Glen gave me Steve's number before we hung up.

I immediately called Steve to tell him what Johnnie said about the pictures. While I waited for someone to answer, I thought, *Why in the hell didn't Tasha tell me Aunt Dessa had to go to the hospital last night?* Then again, what can you expect from an eleven-year-old? She's probably stressing too. I can only imagine what she must be going through. I'm sure the kids at school are talking about it.

I was too young to realize or care about the male ego, especially the ego of an attorney. My main concern was to do everything I possibly could to get my cousin the help he needed.

"Hi Steve, this is Ontresicia, Glen's, I mean Rodney's, cousin."

"Oh yes, how can I help you?" He said.

"I was talking to Johnnie Cochran and he said to make sure you know to take pictures of Glen because three days had passed and there hadn't been any pictures taken." I said innocently, like a child telling her sibling "Mommy said do this, this, and that."

"I know what to do....I am a personal injury attorney," he snapped.

"Oh...OK. I just wanted to make sure everything was going okay," I muttered. I knew then this would be a long case. He already didn't like me, but like I said, I couldn't be concerned with his ego. After speaking with him, I called Tasha back to inquire about Aunt Dessa's well being. I was sympathetic but I also had to let her know I needed to be contacted if anything happened to Aunt Dessa. Aunt Dessa was not used to calling on the family for assistance since most had been dis-fellowshipped from the faith. Although I was raised in the faith, I had never been baptized, which is a criteria to be dis-fellowshipped when sins are committed. Regardless, she had to be reminded that we were her blood and that she needed to call us in case of all emergency situations. After running errands, I went back to spend some time with her and make sure she was OK.

Finally, time for myself. I made plans to meet my friend, Leticia, for dinner at a restaurant in old town Pasadena. It was extremely crowded as it normally was on Colorado Blvd. Walking toward the restaurant, we spotted each other at the same time coming from opposite directions and waved to get each other's attention. We met in front of the Italian restaurant and embraced in a long hug.

"I haven't seen you in a while. I'm so glad you called me," she said.

"Yes, I know, it's been too long." I pulled the door open and we were seated immediately and handed a pair of menus.

"Your server will be right with you. Would you like to see our wine selection or would you like anything else to drink?"

"Yes," I blurted. "I would like a glass of Chardonnay. Thank you."

She turned to Leticia, "And you, Miss?"

"I'll take the same, thank you."

During dinner, I informed my good friend of what had been happening all week. I began by asking her if she had seen the man who had been beaten by the police on television.

"Yes, girl wasn't that something, I wonder what did he do to make them beat him like that?"

"No one deserves to be beat like that regardless of what they did or what they thought they did," I snapped. She cut her smile short and stared at me, perplexed by my outburst.

"Ontresicia, you know I work for L.A. Superior. You'd be surprised at what some people are saying. You don't know what that man did."

"That man is my cousin." I drew in a deep breath. "Remember I told you I had a very trying week? Well, that's why. I've been trying to help see about my Aunt Dessa, Glen's mom, and making sure he's okay as well."

"Ontresicia, I didn't know. I'm sorry."

"We needed money to get a lawyer and I was calling all these lawyers but no one would help unless my aunt coughed up five thousand dollars just to start working on the case."

"What? Don't they do things on contingency or something like that?"

"Yes, but they wouldn't because they thought he needed to be defended, until that tape was aired. Then everybody and their grandmother wanted to represent him." I lowered my voice and leaned in towards Leticia. "But I'm so worried about the lawyer my aunt hired. He doesn't have a good reputation."

"Girl, he needs Johnnie Cochran." She laughed while shaking her head.

"As a matter of fact I spoke to Johnnie a couple of times this week."

"Really!" The mention of his name seemed to make the case more serious to her.

"My aunt won't hire him because she….well, she has someone else." I decided not to go into the whole Jehovah thing.

"Who's better than Johnnie?" She frowned and threw her hands up as if she wanted to ask me if my aunt was crazy or something.

"People keep calling me telling me we need Johnnie but there's nothing I can do. I know my aunt won't change her mind."

We continued to talk about Glen and conversations I had with other attorneys. I again shared how upset I was and how I needed to make sure he had the best to represent him. Then she blurted out something totally unexpected.

"OK, I know he's your cousin and all, but he's not your child. Why are you so upset and into this?" She was my friend but at that moment I wanted to choke the crap out of her.

"I'm not sure of the bond between you and your family but my cousins are just like my brothers and sisters. That's how we were raised." I quickly shifted to another subject, maybe the weather or something, and stayed clear of the Glen matter after that comment.

The next week, between working, going to school, and studying, I tried to keep close tabs on Aunt Dessa. She was still feeling very stressed so one of her friends had talked her into leaving the city for a few days to relax her mind. I called Glen that Friday evening to make sure he was okay.

"Hey cousin." He sounded strange. "Are you OK?"

"No, I'm bleeding from everywhere," he said.

"Everywhere? What do you mean bleeding from everywhere? Did you call Lerman?"

"I called him, but he didn't call me back yet?"

For the first time, I was in a real panic. "OK. Then call the ambulance." Glen didn't answer. He was being hidden from the public and the family as well which I didn't understand, so he wanted to wait to hear from Lerman before he made a move.

He finally answered. "I'm going to wait a little longer to see if Steve calls."

"I don't think that's a good idea, Glen. What do you mean bleeding from everywhere?"

"You know, all the openings of my body….my nose, my mouth, my ass….everywhere."

I didn't know what to do so I told him I would call him back. I quickly called my mom. As the phone rang, I began pacing the floor back and forth wondering why she hadn't picked up on the second ring.

Finally, she answered, "Hello."

"Hi Mommy, it's Treesa."

"Hi baby, is something wrong?" Moms can always tell when something's wrong, even when you're trying to stay calm.

"Yes. I just spoke to Glen. He said he was bleeding from everywhere! All of his openings!"

"From all of his orifices?" Mom asked.

"That's what he said. What should we do? He called Lerman, but he hasn't called him back." By this time, the entire family knew Lerman wanted to keep Glen hidden from the public.

"Oh my God! You need to get Glen to the hospital."

Being so young, I didn't know how serious this could be, but I knew no one should have blood coming from everywhere. Would I put him in more harm if I moved him from Lerman's hideout? Would Glen even tell me where he was?

"Call your Aunt Dessa," Mom said.

"She's out of town with her friend."

Aunt Dessa felt Glen was safe because…well, he was in the hands of Jehovah, via Rentzer and Lerman.

"Well, you need to get in touch with someone and get Glen to the hospital."

After speaking with my mom, I called Steve's office and spoke with an elderly woman who I think introduced herself as Steve's mom. I'm not really sure, but I remember feeling nauseous and having a sudden jolt of pain come and go in my head. I left a message for him to contact me or Glen and told her that it was urgent.

That evening I called Johnnie, worried because I hadn't heard from Steve yet.

"I don't know why he isn't checked into a hospital," Johnnie said. "Where is Glen?"

"I really don't know. He's not in the same hotel he was in last week. Steve moved him because someone found out the password, and Steve said it was too dangerous to leave him there – he had to move."

"If Steve calls back, have him take Glen back to the hospital and have him checked in and evaluated. Oh yeah, I see that Steve only filed against the state. Let him know that he should file in both state and federal courts."

I called Glen again a couple of times throughout the night to make sure he was okay. He sounded like he was doing better….well, not so much better, but he wasn't panicking.

He said he was passing some blood when he went to the bathroom. The next day Steve called me. "I got your message. You can tell Johnnie, Glen had already been to the hospital that's why he has casts on most of his body, but he went back to the hospital, so he'll be okay. And thanks for Johnnie's message," he said sarcastically. Again he was very bothered with me. Another strike against Ontresicia, but again I didn't care.

"Where is Glen now?" I asked, trying to have a little more authority in my voice.

"Ontresicia, I explained this to you before. I can't give out Glen's whereabouts because it's too dangerous. I have had many threats coming into my office."

I wasn't sure who the threats were coming from. He never disclosed details of that. This confused me because Glen was the victim. Who threatens the victim? But he told me that once he placed Glen in an apartment, he would be able to give me information on his whereabouts. I called my mom to let her know Glen was okay.

Chapter Three
The Perils of An Unjust Society

L ater that day, I decided to go to the library to get some studying done. I grabbed my books and strolled to the car. I usually had my radio stations turned to jazz, R & B, or oldies. "Black Pearl" by Sonny Charles and the Checkmates was playing. I've always loved hearing the lyrics to that song: *"Black pearl, precious little girl, Let me put you up where you belong, Black pearl little girl, you've been in the background for much too long..."* It's sad, I thought, that today we, as black women, are not used to hearing such uplifting lyrics about us anymore. I glanced down to check the station; and to my surprise, it was the R & B station where I had never heard that song before. When the song finished, the DJ said, the song had been requested in honor of the little fifteen-year-old girl shot and killed this morning by a Korean store owner. I couldn't believe what I had just heard. I turned the volume up and listened to the DJ talking to callers.

"I don't know what's going on here. It's been only two weeks since we witnessed the videotape of the Rodney King beating," as most referred to it, "now this?" The DJ reported, "For all of you just tuning in, LaTasha Harlins, a fifteen-year-old girl, was shot and killed this morning by a Korean store owner."

I sat in my car watching the radio as if it were a television – shocked at the news. Tensions hadn't diminished yet from the videotape of Glen being beaten like a slave accused of eyeballing a white woman. Now a child had been killed. But, I think the shocker was that the woman wasn't in jail yet. I tried to get the details but all I could gather was that she was shot in the back of the head as she was leaving a neighborhood store on Figueroa Street in L.A. – shot over a bottle of orange juice.

Just like Glen, there was no logical reason for him to be continually beat like that, regardless of what happened prior to that point. Now this little girl, I didn't care what she had done before the shooting when she decided to walk out of that store. It was over. There's no logical reason for someone to feel threatened, if that child was on her way out, walking away from the store owner.

I had a lot of studying to do, so I selected the CD. I couldn't listen anymore to these crimes. I needed to clear my mind so that I could obtain my four year degree and secure a better position at work so there would be no reason for me to be denied to moving up in the company ever again. Before I drove off, I laid my head against the headrest and remembered my motivation for studying and working so hard.

∞

After my immediate supervisor, Chris, had audited my files to discredit my reputation at the company, his manager, Mr. Cotter, eventually offered me a position as a Senior Buyers Aid as opposed to a Buyer I position. When I asked why, I was told that the requirements for the Buyer I position had changed, and I now needed a bachelor's degree, which I was still working towards. However, another lady in the office had recently been promoted without a degree. There were also rumors that she was Mr. Cotter's mistress. He told me, "Triece, take the position, it's a good compromise for everyone." So I did. I couldn't afford to be out of work, but from that point on, Mr. Cotter, who had in the past claimed he wished his two daughters were as hard-working, self-motivated, and responsible as I, would appear in my cubicle all the time claiming to see how Chris and I were getting along. While in my cubicle, he would run his hands up my legs as he spoke to me. I would say, "Mr. Cotter, you need to stop" in an embarrassed, fearful tone, and would remove his hands from my legs. He practically laughed in my face. I was extremely humiliated by him and the whole situation.

This had become a trend in my life, being used, abused, and humiliated. I felt like I was indebted to him for the new position. Other employees would catch a glimpse of this behavior and the rumors started. I was scared and didn't know what to do or how to make him stop. Meanwhile, the relationship with Chris went from bad to worse, so I was moved to the computer hardware and software group, which was closer to Mr. Cotter's office.

Over the years, I began to recognize his footsteps over anyone else. I could be on a call and hear him walking down the hall. Immediately, my palms became sweaty, my heart would race, and suddenly I'd jump up from my seat before he entered my cubicle to prevent him from touching me while sitting and unable to control the situation. When he'd leave, I'd sit back down as quietly and as still as possible, still trembling, too embarrassed to look up to see if any of my co-workers had witnessed this unwelcomed behavior. I thought, *maybe if I sat really still no one would notice. Why didn't he respect me as he did the other women in the department? What was I doing to cause this?*

In hindsight, I had revealed too much about myself to him over the first couple of years. He knew my parents were far away, I had no support system, and that I was struggling and desperately needed this job. He sniffed out my naivety – my need to survive – and like a sly fox, he awaited the opportunity to pounce. Once he started he never stopped until he retired.

My cubicle was right next door to another good ol' boy who previously had been in a management position, but was demoted and hated all of upper management. One day he came into my cubicle and told me Mr. Cotter thought I was his personal chocolate tart. Then he said, "Honey, one day when he comes in here feeling up your legs, you just need to slap the holy shit out'im. That'll stop him." I had two options: one, slap the shit out of him and get fired, or two, just quit. Neither was a realistic option for me. I needed the job, and I was too scared to quit and go somewhere else and start all over again. Over the years, I had been broken – stripped of all confidence and raped of dignity.

∞

I had to get to a higher position in the company so that I could make some changes in the practices. I started my little Volkswagen bug and was on my way. The injustices that had been forced upon my family and me motivated me even more.

A couple of weeks had gone by since the shooting of LaTasha Harlins and the Korean woman had never been jailed. This enraged the community. Many protests were staged for the little girl. They wanted the store closed for good. Some of the people in the community walked around like roaring lions waiting to devour anyone who even looked as though they were going to disrespect them. That was a big part of this problem – disrespect. Our community felt that no one respected or valued us as a people. Many blacks felt it. When I would go to the barbershops or other places where blacks were dominant, I'd hear people talking about not only Rodney King and LaTasha Harlins but of other injustices that had plagued the black community, like how the "driving while black" (DWB) phenomenon, which was proven by former police officer Don Jackson, was getting out of control.

While driving in Long Beach in 1989, two police officers stopped Don Jackson, gave him a hard time and eventually slammed his head into the windshield. Some accused Don of setting up the incident to prove DWB was real and therefore dismissed its validity. But, others felt that if they had fallen for the bait, didn't that prove his point? In 1990, we had heard of a postman being sent to jail for six months for shooting a dog that attacked him. Now added to these were the Rodney King beating and the killing of Latasha Harlins. The community was angry, boiling inside, waiting anxiously to see what would happen to these violators of justice. What would their punishment be?

The investigations of our department at work were still proceeding and I too wondered what the punishment would be for the managers who had discriminated against us as well.

The acts of a subdued, hidden racism were now seeping through the fibers of America, like it had at my job – naked and unfolding everywhere: in the neighborhoods, in Corporate America, in the police force against fellow officers. Though this wasn't new, it was new to me, because I was seeing everything in a different light now. Our lives seem to have no value to America. We were still viewed as mere descendents of slaves, no matter how much education we attained.

It had been months since Glen's tragedy with the police. I had been out of my normal exercise regimen, so I decided to take advantage of the lingering daylight to go for a run. It would be good for me. After my Statistics class, I headed for the track. As I passed some black students, I heard one of the girls say, "You see how they let that lady just kill that girl." One of the guys responded to her but by then I was out of normal earshot range so I heard mumbling and then a loud, "…she was black!" I began jogging to get to the track faster. On the track, I ran fast, jogged some, and power walked for about an hour. I grabbed my backpack and ran to my car. I didn't want to take any chances of hearing anything else. I was overwhelmed with thoughts.

Once home, I bolted for the shower, and stood motionless as the hot water soothed my tense body. After what seemed like the longest shower I ever had, I wrapped a towel around me and collapsed on my bed. I looked at the pictures of Sarah Vaughan and Dorothy Dandridge on my wall and thought of the strength these women had to have back then. I guess each generation had to struggle for the next. We had so many pioneers; now it was time for us to be the pioneers for the next generation. But what angered me was the mentality of some of our youth – that this was the end of the twentieth century and some of our youngsters still didn't understand what Dr. King and Malcolm X represented in our lives.

I felt the same sharp, stabbing pain in my heart from these injustices as the black community did now. Everyone that cared about me, including Johnnie, told me to hold my composure and stay calm. Someone had to stay calm and hold it all together. Yep, that's what everybody told me. This was becoming difficult for me, to such an extent that I was beginning to suffer anxiety attacks and insomnia. Still, I continued to wear my mask of calm and composure.

I closed my eyes for a while. Suddenly, I was awakened by a knock at the door. It was Friday evening and I wasn't expecting anyone. I grabbed my robe and ran to the door, hoping I would be able to get rid of whoever was there quickly. I peeked through the peephole and was relieved. I quickly turned the deadbolt lock and swung the door open.

"Hi Jen. Come on in!" Jen was a friend who lived in the same building. Our work schedules kept us from spending too much time together, and lately, I hadn't been around too much anyway.

She stepped in and hugged me. "Hey girl, how are you doing?" I shut the door behind her and guided her to the kitchen.

"I'm good, how's everything with you?" I answered as I pulled two wine glasses from the cabinet. I wanted to pour my heart out but I had learned through years of experience that sometimes your friends don't or cannot understand your pain, so why bother trying to explain. Besides, I wanted to take a night off from thinking about Glen, JPL, school, and family.

"Oh girl, same old thang. I got home a little earlier tonight so I thought I'd come by and check on my friend. So much has been going on. The more I hear about that little girl…and then they always bring up your cousin's beating too. Are you sure you're okay?"

"I am, and you know what?" I said as I poured wine into our glasses, "I really don't want to think about it tonight. Let's plan a shopping trip. Tell me where the sales are or something. Let's just keep it light."

Jen raised her glass. "Here's to great sales and good shopping."

I laughed and raised my glass, "To shopping." It was nice to have that release from the pressure. Jen and I talked and laughed for a couple of hours before she left. It was still kind of early so I decided to call Glen. I hadn't spoken to him all that week. The last time I spoke to him he was very concerned about the emotional stability of the family, especially his mother.

"Hey Glen, it's Treesa. How are you doing?"

"Hey cous, I'm good. Have you seen Mommy lately?

"Yes, I went by the house a couple of days ago. She seemed okay."

"Oh, OK. I talk to her but I'm never sure if she's really okay or not." He didn't sound too good. Although his woman was with him, I was still concerned about his health.

"Are you still passing blood?"

"It happened a couple of times, but I think it has stopped now. That time when I told you about it…what frightened me was that I could barely hold my own weight up because of the casts and body wraps, so I was just paranoid of anything really going wrong. They said I had a lot of internal damage."

"Oh, well did they say you would have permanent damage?"

"You know what, cous? I don't even remember if they said that or not."

"You sound sleepy so I'm going to get off the phone so you can rest."

"I took a pain pill and I'm just drowsy. As a matter of fact, I think I took a few of them. I'll talk to you later, cous."

"OK, bye."

45

I searched my CD collection for my Spyro Gyra, Steely Dan, old Al Jarreau, Pieces of a Dream, and Alex Bugnon. I placed them all in the CD changer and turned the volume down. I didn't want to think about school, but the reality was I had to stay up on my studies or I would get behind. All too often I'd see so many students at the beginning of a difficult class and then we'd end up with only a few of us there at the end of the quarter. I was determined not to be one of those who had to withdraw or drop a class.

As I organized my books on the table to study, I couldn't help how the conversations in the community had changed. Before the Rodney King beating and the killing of Harlins, I'd often listen to black people having discussions about race and race relations. It never ceased to amaze me how often I would hear someone say, "Oh, my family isn't all black. My grand or great-grand mother was full-blooded Cherokee and my granddaddy's daddy was Irish." It was as though people, black people, were trying to run away and shed their blackness while simultaneously being beaten and stripped of value and dignity in America. It was as though "Africa" and "African-American" were bad words. Blacks spoke as if they had experienced this Native American or Irish culture. Of course, not all blacks, but most of them that I knew would make these comments. But believe me, after the Rodney King and Latasha Harlins incident, everybody became "all" black again.

Now I heard, at the bus stations, in restaurants, hair sa-lons…everywhere I went, about the injustices and plights of black people from the trans-Atlantic slave trade to now. We argued that foreigners had no respect for us and that they had bought into the American stigma of black people. The Koreans, too, felt they could come over into our communities, start businesses, fill their tables with food that came from the money of poor black people, and then shoot our children when the day went wrong for them!

Our community was inconsolable when we found out that a child had been shot in the back of the head – and over a bottle of orange juice? Why hadn't Soon Ja Du been arrested? She was out on bail awaiting her trial. Shouldn't the judge have declared "no bail" for her like they had for most of our crimes? My God, she had shot a child in the back of the head. But of course, they said she was no threat to society. That infuriated the black community even more. How could a woman who shoots a child in the *back* of the head, not be a threat to society? No, the truth of the matter was that since it was just a black child, Soon Ja Du wasn't a threat to society. This was the feeling of most in the community, especially the young people.

Although I knew about racism, it had always been something remote and distant from me. My family fellowshipped and socialized mainly with other Jehovah's Witnesses. We went to school together and played together – all ethnicities. I know it sounds strange coming out of my mouth, but I didn't really see color, or I should say, pay attention to it. If I was wronged in any way, it was because that person was just not a nice person – I didn't feel it could be due to the complexion of my skin. But JPL's transparent decisions, comments, and attitude woke me from that bogus reality.

Chapter Four
April 29, 1992 – Not Guilty!

"They let them go! They got acquitted! The police officers got acquitted everybody!" Two young brothers were yelling and flailing their arms in impassioned frustration.

"All of the police officers were acquitted," they said in astonishment, shaking their heads and laughing sarcastically.

When I heard them, I stopped suddenly and watched. I had just completed my second lap around the field. At first, everyone paid close attention to their announcements but they all kept a safe distance from them. They had walked out of the weight room. There were televisions throughout the gym. I figured they must have heard a special report about the acquittal. Seemed as if everything and everyone around me stood still as I watched and listened to the brothers, both sporting long gym shorts – one with a muscle t-shirt and the other in a sweatshirt.

At that time, African-Americans made up only 1% or so of Cal Poly Pomona's student population. A large group hustled around the track and the gym. I can't remember how many blacks were in hearing distance, but I don't think there were more than four or five of us. Many Asians and a few Latinos passed by watching the young men talking with each other, almost expecting them to get rowdy or something. But they didn't. They were just loud and animated.

My feet were cemented into the asphalt and for several minutes, I couldn't move. My chest began racing again. My body tightened. My spine became rigid and unmovable. The students around didn't seem to care at all. This news seemed irrelevant – unimportant. Before I allowed myself to respond or for time to process the impact this verdict would have on our family, I took off running again, hoping the physical activity would force the verdict out of my head or maybe to break away from the new weight that would surely be added to my already broken-down shoulders. I ran and ran and ran until my physical fatigue finally matched the mental fatigue I had felt for the past year. I finally collapsed on the grass at the edge of the track.

As I stared up at the sky, I realized a couple of things. One, the run didn't help. Two, I was grinding my teeth, which surprised me because just a few weeks earlier, I had insisted to my dentist that I did not grind my teeth despite his insistence that there was evidence I did so at night. I figured he didn't know what he was talking about and I probably needed another dentist. But my jaws were clenched and I was grinding my teeth so hard it was giving me a headache. Was this the manifestation of the anger I had been hiding? The anger I had learned to mask for so many years? This was my first cousin. He had been beaten and victimized by the same people who were mandated to protect us. But to this day, a whole year later, I was probably the only family member who had not watched the tape of the beating in its entirety. The only family member who had not exploded in anger and grief. The calm, cool one. Why hadn't I allowed myself to view the entire videotape? Maybe so I could keep my stoic, emotionless demeanor. Or, so I could remain professional and take care of the business at hand. After all, these things happened all the time, or so I had been told over and over again. Hell, we were lucky Glen was still alive, some would say. But now I was angry. Was I finally allowing myself to feel normal – to feel the anger I had the right to feel?

Finally, I managed to pull myself up from the grass and force myself to take that long, dreadful walk to the parking structure. As I strolled across the campus, it was business as usual. No one cared that Glen had been beaten last year, in March. No one cared that the police "caught on tape" were acquitted. No one cared about the miscarriage of justice or the message society was again sending loud and clear – that black life was of no value. The jury basically told us that we didn't see what we thought we saw on the tape – what many Americans saw on the tape?

I hopped in my bug and jetted down the 60 freeway. Within minutes, I was in the Antiques district on 3rd Street and pulling into my apartment complex. I raced past the decorated turquoise railing toward my quaint one bedroom apartment, anxiously jiggled my keys into the lock and pushed the door open. I dropped my purse and books on the kitchen table, and headed straight for the shower. I knew I would be receiving phone calls soon. Before getting into the shower, I peaked at my answering machine. Flashing lights indicated three new calls. In the shower, I took in several deep, calming breaths and allowed the hot water to rain down on my worn body. After drying off and massaging my arms and legs with my favorite body cream, I wrapped myself in my robe and poured a much-needed glass of chardonnay before dealing with the calls. I had grown accustomed to a nightly "taste" to knock off the edge and to get some sleep. It was not that I was becoming an alcoholic or anything like that, but just a few sips to breathe a little better.

With glass in hand, I turned on the television to see if I could catch some news about the acquittal before listening to my messages. As I clicked the play button to hear messages, a flash from the television caught my attention.

Breaking News. It had begun. KTLA News was reporting on a pre-recorded scene. The police had barricaded themselves in a building, the Parker Center, and locked the door. Some of the protestors were trying to talk, but the excitement of the crowd escalated. The protesters started throwing rocks and yelling at the police while constantly shouting, "Guilty! Guilty! Guilty!" I thought, *that's really bold. I mean, police have guns, they can shoot them or lock these people up, what are they thinking?* Then I noticed, these weren't just blacks protesting; there were different races out there. Cars were being tipped over and set on fire. Other news outlets were now reporting other fires. My head was spinning. I called Aunt Dessa, but there was no answer.

Then, KTLA News reported rioting in L.A. at the corner of Florence and Normandie. I was shocked at what I was seeing. Before I could even fathom what was really going on, more news broke, and I saw my people out in the streets throwing bottles and bricks at cars, and then someone being pulled out of the car and beaten...then another one being pulled out and beaten. My mouth dropped. *Where the hell are the police now?* I thought. The announcer said this was live. *If I'm watching this, I'm sure some nearby police officers have had enough time to respond. Where are they?* I could feel my body trembling, my head beginning to throb, and my stomach turning flips. Suddenly, I jumped when the sound from the phone snatched me out of my trance. I quickly tapped the talk button, "Hello," I said in a panic.

"Are you alright?"

I exhaled deeply and slowly before responding to my mom. "Yes. I was looking at the news, and I feel like I'm in another world right now."

"I know, we've been sitting here watching too. Have you spoken to Dessa? Do you know if she's okay? I tried to call her, but no one answered. The people down there are going crazy like this – over Glen?"

"I don't think this is all for just Glen. I think this is for all the injustices that blacks have endured over time. Glen was just the last straw," I said. As we continued talking and watching the news coverage, I thought, *yep, this verdict was the final chapter of the disrespect, dehumanization, and devaluation of the black community that society had inflicted for decades. Spirits were broken and the people were enraged. We were witnessing the inevitable result of a long-ignored ticking time bomb created by the excessive, unbearable stress that had been forced upon this community.*

As the rest of the world and I sat glued to the television, looking at all of the guiltless people being terrorized, I felt sick. It was like watching a horror movie in which some crazy scientist created a potion and fed it through the main water lines. The people had drunk it and were now running around like zombies, terrorizing anyone that fell into their path.

As I watched, paralyzed, I became increasingly angry and confused. What were we doing? These innocent people had done nothing wrong. I had strong feelings towards the injustices that had overwhelmed our community as well as in Corporate America, but this wasn't the way to handle it. I too, was angry for the way we were treated. By 1992, I had come to realize and feel the racism that was so prevalent in our community. I wasn't what some considered "ghetto". I didn't look or act hard or thug-like in any way. I was just black. Some whites, some Koreans, and other ethnic groups treated me like I was someone that needed to be watched, someone that couldn't be trusted. But I had done nothing to warrant that distrust. I heard about our young men being harassed by the police. I feared for my family and for my young male cousins. I've witnessed injustices in my face daily. Therefore, I understood the rage the community was feeling…the boiling inside of this pressure cooker that had just exploded. I clearly understood the lashing out of the young and old. This was not just about Rodney G. King; this was about Latasha Harlins, Don Jackson, and Floyd Sterling, the postal worker who had been sentenced to jail time for shooting a dog that was attacking him. This was for all of the injustices that we didn't know about, but that these families knew of…the ones who weren't fortunate enough to have cameras around.

On the news, they were calling these people thugs. Some were, but some were just people who were expressing the same thoughts and the same feelings of rage at the same time. A deadly combination. Hundreds of people were running in the streets and pulling people out of their cars. After the victims were on the ground, the rioters would throw bricks and rocks at them or start kicking and stomping them.

As the evening went on, the looters ran through the small mom-and-pop stores, smashing windows, stealing, and then setting fires.

The rioters seemed to target the Korean-owned stores. Some rioters actually passed the stores they knew were black-owned, but some of the black-owned stores got caught up in the mix too. This made me sick. I was grateful to see some blacks intervening in the midst of the mayhem, jeopardizing their own safety to help others get away from the threatening mobs. I had never witnessed anything like this.

I sat transfixed by the actions playing out before me on the television. The rioters were literally in the middle of the street checking the race of the drivers of the cars. God help them if they were not black. I saw a young man waving a few cars through while throwing large stones at others. Then, the angry mob joined in on the attack. Throwing huge bricks or concrete at the windows as the drivers tried to flee. One car tried to speed through the crowd. It swerved to avoid hitting another car, but ended up hitting the car and was stopped sitting in the middle of the turbulence. Of course, the crowd wouldn't attack a person who had just had a collision, I thought. But I was wrong. They ran toward the car, pulled the person out, and began beating him in the face. Thank goodness he could run. He fled, leaving his crashed car behind as the crowd continued throwing rocks and anything else they could find at the man.

I didn't know how much more I could take. There was a man pulled out of a white truck and beat and kicked every time he attempted to get up. Hadn't these people been listening to the news? Didn't they know to take a detour? Obviously not. Then I saw the worst of all. A white man was pulled out of a big red truck. He was severely beaten by about four young black men. He tried to stand after a couple of blows to his body before collapsing onto the street while the young men kicked him over and over again. One of the men threw a huge piece of cement at the victim's head while he laid there bleeding and seemingly unconscious. What I saw then with the rest of America was totally shocking. The young man then pranced around as if he were doing a celebratory dance for his winnings. By now, I was dizzy, nauseous, and feverish with disgust.

I was so angry, but at whom? The rioters? The police who got acquitted? Glen's lawyers for not doing a good enough job? My aunt who wouldn't let Johnnie Cochran handle the case? The jury that saw the entire tape and still acquitted the police? Or angry at the society whose tolerance of police brutality and injustices towards our people who had made all of this possible? Maybe I was just angry at everyone for the cruelty and blatant racism I had experienced for years at my job. I didn't know what to do or think anymore. I thought I would have heard from Johnnie that evening but I didn't. I turned the television off because I needed to think. I needed to get all of that out of my head.

The next morning when I awoke, although my mind was consumed and my body was tense, a peculiar quiet had settled in. I didn't want to interrupt the strange serenity of the atmosphere, but I was drawn to the television, curious to hear what happened as I slept through the night. The first thing I heard was that most of the businesses were closed, even in Pasadena, which surprised me, until I learned that the destruction had begun to travel into various areas of Los Angeles County. Had this gone on all night?

Around noon, the phone rang. I started not to answer because frankly I was tired of thinking, hearing and discussing the verdict, but I peeked at the caller ID and quickly answered.

"Hello Ontresicia," Johnnie said. In his fast-talking, hyperexcited voice he continued without hesitation. "Montel Williams wants to interview someone from your family. I thought of you because I've heard Rodney's auntie on television over the past year, and I just don't think she's a good representation of you and your family."

He was talking about Ann King, Glen's father's sister. Johnnie had grown fond of the strong, calm demeanor I displayed to him over our many phone conversations, but really I was falling apart at the seams. I was just good at hiding it.

"OK. I just need to contact Glen to let him know. I don't think he'd mind."

"No problem. I'll wait for you to call me back before I contact them."

"OK. When did they need me there?"

"I'll have them call you with the details after you check with Rodney."

"OK. Bye." I called Glen as soon as I hung up with Johnnie. I always checked with him prior to making any kind of comments on his behalf. Besides, I wanted to see how he was doing after the riots had broken out. The phone rang several times before he answered.

"Hey Glen, it's me Treesa. How are you doing?"

After a long, heavy sigh he answered, "I'm okay, but cousin, everybody is going crazy out there. I know you've seen the news. I can't stand this. Did you see that man that got pulled out of his truck and beaten like that? I mean, what is this about....really? I just want this to go away."

"I know. This is not fair to these innocent people. But look, I was actually calling you because Johnnie had just called me. The Montel

Williams show would like to interview someone from the family and Johnnie wanted me to go. Are you OK with that?"

"Yeah. I want you to go for me cousin, but be very careful about what you say because the civil trial is going to start soon."

Steve Lerman had already informed Glen of his plans to take this to civil trial if the police were acquitted. "I know Glen, I will be careful. Maybe I should speak to Steve before I go to make sure of what I can elaborate on and what I can't."

"That's a good idea. When do they want you there?"

"Johnnie is going to have the producers call me with the details. I'll let you know as soon as I know."

"OK. Be safe cousin. Talk to you later."

Then I called Steve and told him that I would probably be on the Montel Williams show and wanted to know what I should and should not say. He informed me that he would be there also so I didn't need to worry about answering any difficult questions. I was relieved because I really didn't have any details anyway.

Chapter Five
Montel Williams Show

T he Montel Williams show made arrangements for me to fly out the next day. I was embarrassed to tell them that I had nothing to wear on the show. Most of my business suits were still in the dry cleaners and the businesses had been closed due to the rioting. They were so nice. They asked me about my size and said they would have an outfit there for me.

As I sat in the airport waiting to board the plane I thought about JPL and how the outcome of the investigation had affected us. The group that filed the complaints, had been divided. They had spoken with select people, with whom they resolved salary inequities by making pay adjustments and issued back pay to some, but I wasn't one of them. I was told that I had received two raises a year for most of my career there, which was true, and that they didn't owe me anything. I argued that I had witnessed several people get promoted without degrees, and I didn't. "The policy had changed by the time I had the required years on the job," they said without an ounce of compassion. They also apologized for some of the things I was subjected to earlier in my career, but so much time had passed, that the statute of limitations had expired. By the time the complaint was fully addressed, Mr. Cotter had retired.

In addition to the pay adjustments, three more blacks were hired. To correct the allegation that there were no black managers, one was hired as a Section Manager, I'll call him James, one as a Group Supervisor I'll him call Ken, and the third would be groomed as a Contract Negotiator, I'll call her Janiece. She was given the opportunity to negotiate huge deals, larger than any of us had been given the chance to negotiate. It was a slap in our faces because their resolution did not include us. In fact, I got the feeling that most of us who complained were classified as troublemakers. However, those who were paid were satisfied and wanted nothing further to do with pushing to improve the practices of JPL. It was the oldest trick in the book. Divide and conquer.

At the Montel Williams studio, everything seemed to be going so fast that I barely had time to think. Cameras and lights generated a disturbing heat everywhere. On stage, I sat with Pooh, one of the two men in the car the night Glen was pulled over and beaten, along with Montel. Lerman appeared via satellite. I wasn't prepped prior to the interview so I just kept in mind not to say anything that would jeopardize the civil trial.

The crew performed a couple of sound checks with Montel and powdered the top of his head. Before I knew it, it was lights, camera, and action. The audience clapped as the theme music played. Montel was so warm and sympathetic to what our family was going through. He asked about our mental state and how we were holding up, especially Glen. Then he showed the infamous taping of the beating of Rodney King on March 3, 1991. I sat there watching the video in an enhanced format in its entirety for the first time. Unbeknownst to anyone in the audience or Montel Williams, after more than a year, I had never seen the entire tape. I kept thinking to myself, *Keep it together, don't cry, don't show any emotion, and please God whatever happens don't let this be the place where I finally break down.* Glen and Johnnie were depending on me to do a good job in representing our family.

Montel asked me how I felt when I watched the videotape. *Oh no, I thought, I have to talk about my feelings?*

I answered, "Well, as you and most of the world can see clearly from that video, my cousin was still being beaten after he was on the ground and obviously too hurt to be of any threat to those police officers."

I paused because I really didn't know what happened that night. Thank goodness Steve was there, even if it was via satellite. When Montel asked me questions I couldn't answer, Steve jumped right in and took over. Glen's friend, Pooh, told his version of what happened that night as well. I felt thoroughly confused, nervous, and anxious but tried to stay composed.

Montel shook his head and said, "This is appalling. I can't even begin to imagine what your family must be going through." He then turned to his audience and said, "Ladies and gentlemen, regardless of what he had done prior to the police stopping him, this is unacceptable." We then went to a break. When the break was over, Pooh and Lerman answered most of the questions that they were allowed to answer, and I pretty much gave an account of who Rodney King was before he nearly had the life beaten out of him by the policemen. And that was the end of that.

I had been requested to appear on Montel Williams, did the show, and returned back home - all within a 48-hour time frame. The whole experience went by like a big blur.

Upon returning, I was happy they had arranged a car for my transportation to and from the airport, but as I sat in the huge plush leather fully equipped black limousine, my heart was heavy thinking about the devastation the city was going through – and even worse, what my cousin was going through. The pain he must be feeling to see all of these innocent people being hurt because of him. I knew from our last conversation that he was enduring the weight of this whole catastrophe by himself. The driver asked, "Do you want to drive through the city to see how it looks now?"

"Is it safe?" I asked.

"Yes. There's still a curfew for the city but the major stuff has slowed down."

"Yes," I answered but was unsure if I could handle it. Instead of turning onto the 405 freeway from Century Boulevard, he continued west until he reached Normandie. As we approached the smoldering streets of Florence, the heat inside of my body rose. The window suddenly came down. I guess the driver wanted me to get a real good look. This neighborhood was not as I knew it. It was eerie, like I was floating into the Twilight Zone. A few people were sweeping broken glass and charred remnants from the front of their stores and it seemed everyone moved in slow motion. Some of the businesses had boarded up the windows with the words "Black Owned" written on them. They had realized it was the Koreans that had been targeted. Rumor had it that some of the Koreans placed a "Black Owned" sign on their stores too in order to keep them safe from the rioters.

A man looked toward the limousine, and the look of hopelessness in his eyes was more devastating than the shattered glass, the partially burned, tagged buildings, and the smell from the fires that had overtaken our city a couple of days before.

"It's pretty bad out here, huh?" the driver asked.

"Yep," I whispered. As I gazed out of the window, looking at the destruction, my heart started fluttering and beating so fast it seemed it was skipping beats. I gasped for air as a surge of heat rushed over my face. My muscles went limp as my stomach decided to do somersaults and my eyes began to fill with a blanket of tears, which blew away from the wind blowing in my face. I wiped the one tear that had managed to fall to my cheek.

I thought, *Who's going to protect him from this calamity?* This was the question Johnnie Cochran, who had become my daily telephone confidant, posed to me almost nightly as he too was caught up in the frenzy of anxiety from the previous year. Within the last year, anyone and everyone could feel the sadness, anger, hostility and misdirected hatred between all races. It felt like a revolution. Since the majority of our aunts, uncles, and first cousins resided in northern California, I had accepted the responsibility that my new telephone confidant had requested of me – to protect Glen and represent our family in a positive light.

While I was in New York, at the taping, I heard of other riots breaking out all over the country. There was one in Tampa, Florida and another in Las Vegas. As I sat there, I wondered how those cities looked now.

I would do my best to stand up and protect Glen – become his big sister, since in my heart that's what I had always been anyway. Since the beating, I worked even harder – not only to save him from himself, but also from this menacing society. This was too big for me.

I was tired. My mind was tormented with many thoughts. I felt the need to just run.

I thought about the emergence of the new hip-hop culture and how these new rap groups were shouting out to America what they were feeling. Back then, hip-hop music was getting more recognition than ever with high-profile groups like NWA. Their lyrics expressed the treatment of African-American youth in L.A., the hard living conditions, the economic disparities, and the hopelessness they felt. In 1991, after the killing of Latasha Harlins, Ice Cube wrote a song called "Black Korea," which I believe he wrote to express the treatment of blacks by Koreans. I wasn't really into rap at that time but even if I was, this song would have still offended me. The lyrics were so harsh and threatening. Being black in America has never been an easy task, but this would only make things worse. Besides the profanity, the lyrics generalized all Koreans as the same. The same way a lot of other ethnic groups did to us. Although some of the lyrics, I could relate to as mentioned before like, "Thinkin' every brother in the world's out to take, So they watch every damn move that I make." But the words, "So pay respect to the black fist or we'll burn your store, right down to a crisp" left a bad taste in my mouth.

The lyrics of these rappers spoke to America in a way that Dr. Martin Luther King would have opposed. I, too, opposed these lyrics, though I was being subjected to the same treatment, but in a different environment. There was a proper way to fight and express our feelings, and this was not it.

The Republicans had been in office for a long time. The party seemed disengaged from the needs of underprivileged communities – especially black communities. Interest rates were sky high. There was superflation. People were hungry, and their only means of survival seemed to be slang'n, hustl'n, and gang bang'n. Our streets were filled with rock cocaine, stories about mothers abandoning and selling their babies for rocks and signing the deed to their houses to the dope man. Grandparents were forced to hang on past their normal life expectancy in order to raise a set of grand or great-grandchildren. It was a horrible time. How could I have been so desensitized? Was it because right out of high school I had been inducted into white Corporate America? Was it because in my new environment, I was surrounded by middle- to upper-white America? But it's not like I socialized with these people outside of work. Besides, I was struggling to survive financially and they weren't. Not only had I learned not to show my feelings; but I was beginning not to feel at all…until now. Looking back I think it pained me too much to look at it intimately, for what it really was. So I mentally pushed it from my thoughts – from my reality.

Chapter Six
"Can't We All Get Along?"

F inally, I was back in my little apartment, safe and sound from the world. I hadn't spoken to anyone since I had arrived back from the show. It was nice being in my serene surroundings again. I placed the small carry-on in my bathroom and opened the patio door to let some air in, but closed it immediately when I smelled the stench of the fires still burning.

I kicked off my shoes and turned on the television to see what was going on. It was the third day of the riots and though some places were still experiencing disturbances, things were starting to settle down. There were thousands of troops in L.A. CNN was showing the troops stomping around in their combat gear. Oh yeah – they meant to put the Negroes back in line tonight.

I went over to the fridge hoping I had something in it to eat. I couldn't remember when I had last visited the market. I hadn't had much of an appetite for months. Just what I thought, nothing in the fridge. I decided to order some food. Chinese or pizza? Exhausted, I plopped down in the chair in front of the television. Then I heard it. "Breaking News." I thought, *what now?*

My heart dropped to the bottom of my gut as my body tensed up to prepare for another tragedy. Then I saw Glen on the television speaking out for the first time. CNN reported, "The man who had become the unwilling symbol had decided to speak out." Seeing Glen out there in the open, vulnerable to the world, I wanted to cry. I could hear in his voice he was nervous and all choked up. He didn't want any of this. He forced out the words, "I just wanna say, um…Can we all get along?" While stuttering he repeated again, "Can we all get along? Can we stop making it harder for the older people and the kids?" That was the Glen I knew and loved. His first comments were about the older generation and the younger generation. We were taught to always respect our elders and everyone was always supposed to look out for the young. He nervously spoke about the L.A. smog and how we didn't need to add to it with these fires. I wanted to be there with him to give him a big ol' hug. He said, "They won the battle, but they haven't won the war…." He fought back the tears as he spoke about a security guard that had been shot…just lying on the ground. That's just what this mess had become – a war. Although, Glen was no angel, he was a decent person and seeing all of those innocent people being slaughtered in the streets bothered him.

A little later, I called Aunt Dessa to check on her and Tasha. "Hi Aunt Dessa, are you okay? I just got back from New York and wanted to check in with you."

"Yes, Auntie is okay, baby. Did you see Glen on the television?"

"Yes Auntie, I saw him."

"I hope nobody does anything to him," she said. "I'm sure he'll be okay." I chatted with her for a little longer and watched Glen on several stations repeating the taped version of his plea for the people to stop rioting and burning down the stores.

The next morning, actor Edward James Olmos rose up as a true community leader by coming out with his broom and cleaning the streets. That kind, gentle gesture provoked others to come out so that the healing process could begin. The weekend was quiet and more people came out to see the damage. Many of the activists and would-be politicians wanted to now look at this community and its issues that had been ignored for years. Many wanted to offer their opinions of why this happened and what the resolution should be.

The Korean community tried hard to patch up their relationship with the black community. I remember during an interview with Korean store owners, the reporters asked them about their store policies to confirm, I guess, what some blacks had shared with the reporter. For example, how they wanted cash only, no refunds, and no exchanges policy to the black customers. The Korean owners said they would look into those policies and possibly change them. I think some of them were realizing their part in the continued injustice the community had felt and had been feeling for years. I'm sure they weren't all bad – just a few. The problem was the few made it bad for the majority.

The following Monday, I was back at work. I wasn't happy from the outcome of our complaint from months ago. As I matured and understood just how wrong I had been treated in the past, the sight of JPL made me sick.

Ten years had passed since I first stepped through the doors of JPL. When I started, all I wanted to do was please everyone by doing a good job. I had no parents to talk to for guidance, no one I could talk to about certain intimate issues that most young girls needed to discuss with their moms. Not only was I out here alone, my mom and I weren't seeing eye-to-eye on things, so we weren't really close at that time. Although I lived with my Uncle Wesley in Altadena, it wasn't like having your mom to talk to about certain things. As I slowly sauntered my way through the building, I thought about how I had been mentally and physically abused for years, but that's just life at JPL.

Looking back over my life, I remembered why I really came to Southern California. I had always told people that I came here to attend college, because my past was too hurtful to speak about. When I was a senior, my life at school began to look up, but my family life was falling apart. I was beginning to socialize with scholars as opposed to only the athletes due to my vigorous training in gymnastics. I became active in student government and was preparing for college. It was an exciting time for me, but my mom didn't share in my enthusiasm. Her idea of college was to take a few bookkeeping classes. My mom had raised me to be someone's wife. She felt educated people looked down at uneducated people. I guess that was her experience. At the end of the school year, my parents and I had a falling-out. I'm not sure over what. I probably didn't do something for my siblings, clean the house right, or was not where they wanted me to be at the exact time they wanted me to be there. I don't really remember, but I was stressed over finals and college tests, so for the first time I stood up to them. My mom was livid. The fear she had instilled in me was gone.

The next week was graduation, and my parents were still so angry that they said they would not be attending my graduation. Truly, I felt I hadn't done anything wrong, but they saw my speaking up for myself as total disrespect for them – and that was something no child would ever be permitted to do. This was my graduation, how could they not come? I was devastated.

On the day of graduation, my mom's cousin Charles saw me walking down the hill on my way to the ceremony.

He said, "Motor," a nickname he called me, short for "motor mouth."

"Where you going all dressed up?" he yelled out of the window of his black Z28.

"I'm going to my graduation."

"You can't make it to that school on time with those high heels on." He took a sip of his beer wrapped in the brown paper bag and said, "Get on in this car." So I quickly hopped in the front seat and he drove me to my graduation.

Later, my cousins, Sherry and Troy, told me that they went by our house and got my mom to come with them to my graduation. I didn't know when I walked across the stage she was there but when I found out, I felt pure joy. I thought everything would be better then.

About a week later, my mom called my Uncle Wesley and asked him if I could stay with him for a while. He said "yes" and came and got me. My plans for attending college in Northern California were over. My mom told me it would be best for me to leave. She said perhaps if I was away for awhile, I'd learn to appreciate our family.

So walking into this place on Monday after witnessing my cousin, for over a year, being humiliated, beaten and stripped of human dignity once again, I was in no way ready to see the two-faced, backstabbing, sorry-for-an-excuse women and the good ol' boys, carrying on and making comments about my cousin.

I finally made it to my desk and began my day. I worked hard and fast – most of the time feeling like I was in another body at work. I was a machine. I was numb, as if in a trance. That was my way of coping and protecting myself. I survived that day and the days to follow just as I had been surviving since I started. Thank goodness it was Friday.

The new black employees kept their distances from the rest of us during the work hours. I guess they wanted to show the good ol' boys they could be trusted overseers. But on payday, Friday nights, we'd usually all see each other at the local happy hour spot, called Menage, located on Colorado Boulevard in Pasadena. It was owned by a group of black men, one of whom also worked at JPL. So after the long week, I decided to go hang out and have a drink to ease my mind. There, everybody drank, complained, and talked work politics. Hell, I needed to vent too. But after the divide, you really didn't know who to trust at that point. When I arrived that evening, the newly hired black supervisor was complaining about how ignorant and ghetto the people in L.A. were during the riots. I thought, *This is probably going to be a short night for me,* until I noticed a couple of my friends that were supportive and sympathetic of my family and me. I ordered a drink and sat down in one of the empty barstools near my friends. When the supervisor, Ken, saw me, he said seemingly extra-loud, "I couldn't even get to work on time. I felt like I was putting my little boy in danger just to try to get him to the babysitter's house." He said this looking at me as though it was my entire fault.

Then the new contract negotiator, Janiece, wanted to join the "let's humiliate Triece" contest, and chimed in with, "So Triece, what's so important about your cousin?" She shrugged her shoulders as she lifted her glass and continued, "OK, so he got beat up by the police, it's not like he's a martyr; in fact, I'd say he'll go down in history as the most infamous person." She laughed as she took another sip of her white wine. I didn't dignify her idiotic comment with a response. I just looked at her and thought how she wouldn't even be in my face if we hadn't fought for her to be here. *How stupid are you?* I thought. I took a sip of wine while the daggers flew from my eyes to hers. I wanted so badly to get up and just beat the crap out of her, but that would only confirm their conviction that my family and I were ghetto. The entire situation started to affect me. I would hear people snickering and bickering about Glen. Sometimes it was embarrassing for me. They were really laughing at me and my entire family.

The next morning, Glen called. "Hey cous, I need to talk to you. Can you come over this evening?"

"Sure. Where are you now?"

"I'm in some apartments in the valley."

"OK. I'll come later this evening." We chatted for a little while about the family. I wrote down the address and hung up. I was excited and looking forward to seeing Glen. Although we had talked often, I hadn't seen him since all of this started.

I drove down the 134 freeway, exited Vineland, and followed the directions he had given me. I spotted the address and began looking for a parking space. I remembered seeing a liquor store on the corner. I parked, climbed up the stairs to the security gate, and pushed the button for Glen's apartment. He buzzed me in.

He was on the second floor towards the back. The courtyard was well manicured and full of bright rose bushes surrounded by stone benches through half of the complex. Towards the second half of the courtyard was a sparkling midsize pool. The staircase leading to the second floor was to the right in the corner. I climbed up the stairs and Glen's apartment was the third door to the left. I knocked on his door. Glen opened the door with a huge smile. I looked up at his smooth mocha skin, black wavy hair, and deep soulful eyes. He looked down at me, "Hey cousin," he said as he pulled me in, lifting me up as he gave me a big bear hug.

When I went in, his girl Crystal was there. "Hi Crystal," I said.

"Hey Triece," she said, as if she had just seen me yesterday. No "how you doing" or anything. Things weren't great between Crystal and Glen, and she seemed upset that evening. She just sat on the couch with her short dress and fishnet stockings as if she were waiting for someone to pick her up.

"Come in here," Glen said while gesturing me to the kitchen away from Crystal. We both sat at the table and exchanged small talk before I began filling him in on the little things that had been going on in the past year that I hadn't shared in our phone conversations.

"Do you know an attorney named Milton Grimes?" Glen asked.

"No, he never called me."

"Well, Crystal's aunt's husband, who is an ex-ball player, used him. So they think I should fire Steve and hire Milton for the civil case."

"Since you're letting Steve go, why not hire Johnnie?" I argued on behalf of Johnnie because I thought he would be the best person to handle the civil case and he had been so generous in providing advice during the past year. In my mind, he had earned the right to represent Glen in the civil trial.

"Do you think he can work with Milton?"

"I don't know, I'll ask him?'

This was the first time we really had a chance to sit face to face and just talk. We reminisced about childhood, the religion, and everything in between. I said, "Hey cousin, do you have anything to drink?"

"No, but there's a liquor store at the corner. I'll buy something. What do you want?"

"I want some cognac," I said deviously.

"Come on, let's go. I'll give you the money to buy it because Steve and everybody says I'm not supposed to be drinkin', so I can't buy that."

"OK. I will." I devilishly joked about it. I couldn't understand why my cousin couldn't have a little drink. On the way to the store, Glen told me that Crystal was waiting for her cousin to pick her up. When we returned to the apartment she was gone and we both had a drink. It was a good evening; we laughed and continued reminiscing about our childhood and his second child Dene. He loved her so much. We recalled the time when he and his first wife, Dee Dee, had temporarily separated and Glen took the baby because she was a toddler and he didn't want just anybody around his baby girl except our family. He was such a good dad.

I asked Glen, "Do you remember I came over to the house one day and you had Dene sitting on some pillows on the floor while you sat on the couch, scrunched over her trying to comb her hair? It was a hilarious scene, because I remembered how large and awkward your hands were as you attempted to part her hair into four sections. Then you added water and grease on one of the sections and brushed it straight. Now most women would have put a rubber band on the hair first to keep the hair sleek, then wrap the hair ornament, with the two little balls that looked like candy, around the ponytail. But not you. You were set on using the hair ornament as the rubber band. So I laughed at you and said, 'that will never work' and you said, 'yes it will cousin, watch me. I've got this shit down to a science now. Watch.' True enough, over time you had gotten hair combing down to a science because you wrapped that hair in those ornaments and the hair was smooth and sleek." I cut my smile and said, "Dene sat there quiet and still as her daddy finished making her look like a little princess for the day. She looked into your eyes as though you were the only person in her little world who mattered. She was definitely a daddy's girl. I remember you told me, 'Cousin, if DeeDee don't come back, I can take care of my baby. I know how to do everything now. I feed her, give her baths, comb her hair. I don't really need help. I can do it all by myself,' you were bragging hard."

As I reminded him what he had said, he laughed, and then his eyes dropped down to the table. As we took another sip of our cognac, he looked at me and said, "I sure do miss my baby. I haven't seen Dene since I came home from prison. I've been away from everybody for so long. Steve keeps finding me new places to live for protection....but I miss my family."

The last thing I wanted to do that evening was bring my cousin down, so I continued reminiscing about our childhood. I tried to bring up the funniest and best times we had in hopes of lifting his spirits and making sure he remembered that whatever happened, we were family and we were here for him. I reminded him of another time when my mom and I lived in Pasadena with Aunt Dessa and Uncle Ronnie for a short time. Glen was a pretty little boy – a year and a half younger than his brother Gailyn and me. Glen had the big curly loops of hair. You know, a pretty boy; but Gailyn and I were your plain run-of–the-mill black kids with nappy hair. That's what my mom called it back then. So my mom and Aunt Dessa decided they would make my hair and Gailyn's hair curly like Glen's, and off they went to buy a perm kit called "Curl Free." I never forgot it because they said the curl solution would loosen our curls and then we'd look like Glen. They put the solution on my hair first, but it was so nappy that it didn't work that well. As I sat on the hard, cold linoleum countertop in the kitchen, watching their expressions, my mom said, "Ontres' hair is hard and brittle now, feel it Dessa." I remember they looked at each other with a scared, puzzled look on their faces after inspecting my hair. As if to say, "What happened to the curls?"

Now it was Gailyn's turn. You would have thought that from their experience with my hair, they would leave Gailyn's alone. I was removed from the hot seat and sat down next to Glen on the kitchen floor to watch the now very frightened Gailyn get his in-home hair treatment. My Aunt Dessa put the solution on Gailyn's hair and covered it up with a plastic cap. After what seemed to be a short time, probably because Glen and I had started playing, I was startled by Aunt Dessa yelling, "Helen! Helen! Come over here. Blood is oozing from Gailyn's scalp!"

Mom shouted, "Oh my God, Dessa! You better rinse it out." Glen and I looked at each other and started laughing. I guess we were both too young to understand any real harm in any of it.

75

Glen looked at me and started laughing and asked, "Are you serious, Cous? I don't remember that. That's the craziest shit I've ever heard."

We laughed and continued drinking. I said, "Do you remember when me and Gailyn got a whipping because we made you stick that coat hanger into the blown out electrical socket?"

His browed creased and he said, "I kinda remember that one," he said, like that wasn't that funny.

We had so much fun talking about old times because Glen had been locked up for some years and when he was released in December 1990, the incident happened shortly thereafter, so I hadn't seen him since he had gotten out. Although I didn't want to bring him down…I didn't want to take him back to that awful night, but I had to ask. I had to finally hear it from his mouth to my ears.

The smile and laughter ceased and I asked for the first time, "Glen, what happened that night of the beating?" He paused for a moment as he gathered his thoughts, and a serious look appeared across his face before he began to speak. "Me, Freddy, and Pooh were coming from that park where Uncle Ronnie used to take us, driving on the 210 freeway. The police put the lights on us but there were no street lights, it was really dark, and that area was known to be a racist area. So I tried to find a lit-up area to stop and that's why I kept going. When I finally pulled over," Glen stretched his hands out shaking his head as he continued, "I did everything the police asked me to do." He took a deep breath and said, "Then I remember they started just beating me and I heard them saying, 'Get down. Get down. Don't move.' I felt like I was going in and out of consciousness, everything was blurry, but I heard them calling me "nigga" while they were beating me. My body was out

Broken Spirits:

of control. I couldn't control my movements, they were tasing me, and my body was jumping uncontrollably, but they kept yelling 'Get down!' while continuing to tase and beat me."

It broke my heart to watch my cousin relive that night. He refilled his glass with more liquor and gulped it down quickly, as if to wash those memories back to that hidden place in his mind. Like I said, I didn't want to take him there, but I had to know. I got the sense that they were making his body jump intentionally so they could continue their sport.

After coming back from his trance, he asked, "What exactly did you say at the Montel Williams show?"

"Glen, I found myself somewhat speechless. It was the first time I had watched the video up close and from beginning to end; and Montel's people had sent the video somewhere, I think he said in South America, to enhance the sound and visuals even more. So I saw the whole beating in detail….enhanced details." I took in a deep breath and continued, "It overwhelmed me so much that I found myself lost for words. I just remembered you telling me not to answer questions directly about the beating because the civil trial had to take place. Besides, I didn't really have any details to tell, other than to describe you prior to the beating. Besides, since Lerman was there via satellite, I didn't have to answer too many questions."

"That's fine, Cous, I'm sure you did a good job."

"But when Pooh was interviewed, his account of the moments leading up to the car stopping was different than what you just told me. What Pooh told Montel was, "me and Freddy was beggin' Rodney to pull over. We told him 'stop, man, stop. What are you doing? Just stop the car.'"

"He's lying. He's got his own agenda right now and it has to do with money, you know what I'm sayin'?"

By now it was in the wee hours of the morning. I took a sip of my coffee and said, "Yeah Cous, I know exactly what you're sayin'."

Chapter Seven
Life After the Verdict

I slept in the next morning since I had spent most of the night with Glen. It was good seeing him again. Around ten-thirty, I dragged myself from the bed and strolled into the bathroom. My head was aching – an unpleasant reminder of how much alcohol I had consumed last night. As I finished washing my face, the phone rang. I dived into my airy, feather down comforter and pillows before grabbing the phone and closed my eyes. "Hello," I whispered. Not to sound sexy but to keep my head from exploding.

"Hello Ontresicia." My eyes popped opened.

"Hi Lois. How are you?" Though I didn't want to excite myself, I was thrilled to hear her voice. I hadn't spoken to her in a while. Lois and her husband, Larry Gammel, were also community activists. Larry was the President of BBA prior to Tyrone Hampton.

"Hey, you sound tired. Did I catch you at a bad time?"

"Not really, I was just out kinda late so I'm just slow getting started this morning." She and her husband were such professionals I didn't want her to know I had been up late just boozing. Though I'm sure she would understand, they were not prudes nor were they judgmental.

"Anyway, I just wanted to personally call you to invite you to a party we're having in a couple of weeks. You'll get the invite in the mail but I wanted to call you to let you know I really wanted you to come. We hadn't had a chance to sit and talk for a while. I need to see you so I will know how my little friend is really doing."

"You're so sweet. I'm okay and I am going to try my best to be there."

"OK. Well, I'll let you get back to your rest. Talk to you soon."

"OK. Bye."

I thought, before I go back to sleep maybe I should call Johnnie to see if he knows Milton Grimes and see if he's willing to work with him on the civil trial. I sighed deeply and figured, why bother him on a Sunday, I'll call tomorrow.

I closed my eyes and tried to get back to sleep, but hearing Lois' voice reminded me of one of the reasons why most of the upper management had taken a strong disliking towards me – another reason why I was seen as a troublemaker.

∞

After I had been at JPL for a while, I started attending the Pasadena/Altadena Black Business Association. The Contractor's Capability Manager, Roger, introduced me to the association. Roger was in charge of the contractor capability department that initially screened the applications from businesses that were trying to be added to JPL's vendors list. I met many black business owners after joining the association. Despite my youth, I felt this passionate desire to acclimate myself to the black community and politics.

As I continued to go to these meetings and listen to the issues, I knew I had to do something to help. They were talking about getting their foot in the door of JPL to bid on contracts – and I was there. With my new role as Senior Buyer Aid, I was in a position to help them; make something happen. I met one of the owners of a raw metals company. He told me he had been trying to get into JPL for years. I took his information and told him I would see what I could do. By now, I realized my tenuous position in corporate America so I had to proceed with caution.

I began to meet the owners of many black businesses – one of which was PB Metals – through Roger. Although Roger was in a management position, he was also frustrated by the many applicants he felt deserved to be on the vendors list. He would screen them and then send the applicants to the buyers only to have them denied time after time. He noticed the white businesses he recommended always seemed to make it to the vendors list, but black businesses that were screened by the same strict criteria were routinely rejected. It appeared there was an unspoken policy not to use black businesses.

After I had obtained all of the information for PB Metals, I told my Senior Buyer, who was a white gentleman, that I wanted to add this vendor to our list. He chuckled and said, "I hope you know what you're doing." Since he had been at JPL for a long time, he too knew the difficulties I would face. He advised, "Make sure you check them out thoroughly." I made absolutely sure the company met every single strict criterion for becoming a vendor. It was a good company but, like many, it was never given the equal chance as its white competitors.

I succeeded and was so proud for my little part in helping my community. It wasn't like I was giving this company something that they didn't deserve. Their products were just as good as any other vendor's. They just lacked the inside connection like their competitors. After using PB Metals for months, one of the engineer liaisons had praised the company's timeliness, professionalism, and quality of their products – but had never seen anyone from the company. Everything was delivered to our shipping and receiving department.

One day, I walked into work and bee-lined straight to my desk. I was running late for our weekly eight o'clock meeting. After the meeting, the same engineer liaison, who I'll call Ted, was expecting a delivery from PB Metals. He followed me to my desk and asked me to let the company know that he would pick up the products we had ordered because he had business out that way, so he would go by. "No problem. I'll call them now." He didn't say thank you, just walked away. That was business as usual here at JPL – no common courtesy. Well, at least not to me and a few others like me.

Later that day, I was very busy and felt overwhelmed. I had just sat down at my desk with a fresh cup of coffee and leaned over to get some papers out of my file when Ted blew in like a twister and began to scold me in his usual tyrannical demeanor. Ted was over six feet tall with a huge nose plastered in the center of a (what we used to call) crater face. His eyes were blue and his teeth were coffee-stained yellow but very straight. He kept his gray and black hair slicked back like truckers. "You know, Triece, we can't contract out to just anyone. We have to be careful about who we do business with. These types of businesses are not responsible or reliable and it's just a matter of time before they screw up and leave you holding the ball."

His comment left me puzzled – a fact I'm sure my expressive face revealed. I closed my file and turned my chair slightly towards him. "What do you mean?" I asked. "This is the same company you have been raving about for months. I don't understand what the problem is. Did something happen?" Instead of responding, he stormed away.

I guess he didn't care for my response or he didn't want to explain why he was so bothered.

Soon afterward, Chris came to my desk and asked me a few questions about the vendor. I answered his questions and asked him what was going on. He chuckled and said, "Ted said 'that nigga bitch think her shit don't stink.'"

I was stunned. First, that Ted had used those words, but then that Chris, a supervisor, would actually repeat it. As you can see, I was still a little naïve. Chris was probably happy to tell me something so awful – especially since he thought I had way too much confidence. Comments to demean us, the few blacks in the department, were heard daily, but not that severe and not that blatant…and in my face. Like I said though, I had by that point become emotionless – stolid to the ridicule and mockery we faced daily from the senior managers, supervisors, and our white counterparts. I had learned to oppress my feelings and deny myself, all for the sake of staying at this prestigious company. Hanging on to the words of the older, mature blacks who constantly told me how good I had it. So much was going on in my career that seemed parallel with the injustices of the community. I was beginning to understand.

∞

I closed my eyes for a little longer before getting up to start my day. I had to learn how to start forcing positive thoughts into my head. I needed to take time for myself and have a little fun again. Life shouldn't be this hard for a young single woman with no children to feed. That was one of my problems – I took on family members' problems as though they were mine. But then again, isn't that what family is for? So I hung out that weekend with my cousin, Debra, and her son, Terrell, and we had a great time.

Monday morning I decided I was going to have a happy day no matter what. I stepped off of the elevator and leisurely walked through the double doors to our department. "Good morning, Susie," I said with a cheerful smile.

She crinkled her face as if she smelled something and said reluctantly, "Morning."

I ignored her already pessimistic attitude and continued walking to my desk, speaking to everyone as I passed by. They probably thought I was on something, but who cared. I looked at my schedule of things I needed to do for the day, made some adjustments, and went to the break room to pour myself a hot cup of coffee. As I was stirring my coffee, I heard one of the manager's from the hallway say sarcastically, "Can we all get along?" and then he and one of my co-workers laughed as they walked into the break room. The laugh was cut short when they saw me standing at the counter stirring my coffee. My eyes stayed on my cup as I continued to stir in the silence of the room. They poured their coffee without a word. I took a sip and walked out. Before I was six feet from the door, I heard an outburst of laughter. So my day didn't go so great after all but I, once again, survived.

That evening after work, I called Johnnie to let him know I had spoken to Glen about hiring him for the civil trial. I told him that Crystal's family had gotten an attorney named Milton Grimes from Orange County and that Glen would most likely hire him for the civil trial; but Glen wanted to know if the two of them could work the case together. Johnnie said he didn't mind working with Milton, but there was no way Milton would be lead counsel. Johnnie said, "I know Milton well and I have a lot of respect for him, but there is no way I'm going to be co-counsel to anyone."

I told Johnnie, "I expressed your interest in the case to Glen, but that's all I can do from this point on." By even mentioning Johnnie to Glen again, I had disobeyed my Aunt Dessa; but I thought to myself, *Why don't we give him the best chance to recover damages that he can get? Why not have the very best attorney?* I told Johnnie I would talk to Glen before hanging up. I really didn't understand why Glen wasn't jumping at the chance of hiring Johnnie.

During the weeks immediately following the riots, the newspapers were flooded with the theories of politicians as to why this catastrophe had taken place. Everyone had an opinion, but the responses of the presidential candidates would be vital to their campaign. Even to those who were not running but wanted to help sway the vote towards their pick for the White House had something to get out to the mainstream.

The New York Times wrote: *"Conversely, President Bush argued that the unrest was "purely criminal." Though he acknowledged that the King verdicts were plainly unjust he maintained that 'we simply cannot condone violence as a way of changing the system....Mob brutality, the total loss of respect for human life was sickeningly sad....What we saw last night and the night before in Los Angeles is not about civil rights. It's not about the great cause of equality that all Americans must uphold. It's not a message of protest. It's been the brutality of a mob, pure and simple.'"* May 2, 1992.

The Los Angeles Times wrote: *"Democratic presidential candidate, Bill Clinton, argued likewise that the violence resulted from the breakdown of economic opportunities and social institutions in the inner city. He also berated both major political parties for failing to address urban issues, especially the Republican Administration for its presiding over 'more that a decade of urban decay' generated by their spending cuts. He maintained that the King verdicts could not be avenged by the 'savage behavior' of 'lawless vandals.' He also stated that people 'are looting because…they do not share our values. And their children are growing up in a culture alien from ours without family, without neighborhood, without church, without support.'"* May 3, 1992.

The Los Angeles Times further wrote: *"In his public statements during the riots, civil rights activist and Baptist minister Jesse Jackson sympathized with the anger experienced by African-Americans regarding the verdicts in the King trial, and pointed to certain root causes of the disturbances. Although he suggested that the violence was not justified, he repeatedly emphasized that the riots were an inevitable result of the continuing patterns of racism, police brutality and economic despair suffered by inner-city residents — a tinderbox of seething frustrations which was eventually set off by the verdicts."* May 4, 1992.

The New York Times wrote: *"African-American Congressional representative of South Central Los Angeles, Democrat Maxine Waters, said that the events in L.A. constituted a 'rebellion' or 'insurrection' caused by the underlying reality of poverty and despair existing in the inner city. This state of affairs, she asserted, were brought about by a government which had all but abandoned the poor through the loss of local jobs and by the institutional discrimination encountered by people of racial minorities, especially at the hands of the police and financial institutions."* May 10, 1992.

As much as I, as well as many other African-Americans, hated seeing these horrific actions displayed on television across the nation, we had to agree that the aftermath of the verdicts of the Rodney King trial exposed the mistreatment of inner city youths around the country. America finally had to take notice and address the issues that had beleaguered our communities for many years.

A couple of days later, Johnnie spoke to someone in Glen's corner, Crystal's aunt. It was made clear to Johnnie that they wanted Milton Grimes to lead the case, so he backed away. But he assured me that Glen was in good hands with Milton. He was a very capable attorney, and my family and I shouldn't worry about anything.

I hadn't been to any of the Black Business Association's events lately, so since Lois had taken the time to personally call me to invite me to a gathering at her home, I decided to go. It was great to get all dolled up for a special occasion. I jumped up Saturday morning and went to the local nail shop for a pedicure and manicure. I hadn't pampered myself in a while. Truth be told, I really didn't have the means to pamper myself on a regular basis, but I tried to give myself a treat once in a while. I started early in the morning so I would have time to get my hair done and still make it home in time so I wouldn't have to rush. Getting your hair done on a Saturday was always risky. I went to Just-In-Time to get my hair done after my manicure. I was lucky because Gina was there and had just finished with a client so I didn't have to wait. From there I jumped in Chuck's chair to get my brows arched and made it back home in time to get myself together without being in a rush. I pulled out this gorgeous royal blue dress that just melted on my every curve. I hadn't had a date in a long time; so maybe this dress would bring me some luck. I laid the dress on the bed, wrapped my hair, and took a quick shower.

Since I hadn't been around for a while, I had forgotten how serene and tranquil their home was. I parked on the street just passed the extra long, full driveway and trotted up the hill to the double glass door decorated with a mix of wrought iron and glass. As I entered the foyer, I was met by a person they had hired for the party. He stood in front of the huge curved staircase, received my jacket, and escorted me to the sunken recreation room, where they had a large pool table to the side of the room and a bar. The other guests were there mingling. This was not just a regular meeting, but it was a celebration of some sort. I can't remember what we were celebrating, but it was big. I had been so emotionally whipped I just wanted to get out and have a good time with people who wouldn't look down on me or would be laughing and snickering behind my back. It was good to just be in the presence again of these outstanding, profes-sional black people. Most of them were much older and wiser than I was. They were the blacks who had made it through the struggles but never forgot from where they came. They lived in their huge homes, drove their fine cars, but still reached back and helped the community. When I entered, I immediately felt some release from the pressure and weight I had been carrying.

"Hey Ontresicia!" Lois said, waving her hands high from behind the small crowd. We met in the middle of the room and embraced, as if she knew I needed a hug – like she could feel my pain.

Clutching my hands, she looked me square in the eyes, and said, "Okay, now let's find a place to talk and I want you to tell me how you're really doing."

I squinted in confusion because there were plenty of guests for her to attend to, so I was surprised she wanted to have a one-to-one with me now. We clasped hands and strolled through the French patio doors over to a quiet, empty little niche in the backyard. We sat on a strikingly gorgeous stone and marble bench against the wall. Lois crossed her legs towards me and asked, "What's really going on with you?"

"Well, it's not much to tell aside from what you've seen on the news." I hunched my shoulders as if that was it. But Lois was not letting me off so easy.

"The news didn't tell me how Ontresicia was holding up through all of this. The news can't tell me if you need a shoulder to cry on." She took my hand into hers and said, "You tell me how you are doing. I want to hear from you….my friend that I care about."

Immediate shame and embarrassment rushed me as I felt tears filling my eyes and rolling down my cheeks before I had a chance to stop this emotion from surfacing. I wiped my face quickly and said, "There's just so much going on. Not just with the family and Glen but at work. I'm just so tired of being treated like nothing. I'm so tired of people telling me this is normal…."

"Wait a minute," she abruptly interrupted. "What are you talking about? Is someone disrespecting you at work?"

I giggled. "Disrespect is an understatement. The people at work talk to all blacks like we are nothing, like we are their modern-day slaves." I explained how one of the managers would rub my legs and the comments he made. How everyone kept telling me that this kind of thing comes with the job. "I'm so sick of hearing that this is normal."

"Sweetie, that is not normal. As a matter of fact, it's against the law. You need to start documenting all of this stuff so you can sue their butts." It was a relief to finally hear that this wasn't something that I should or had to take from this company. I left there feeling vindicated. I felt empowered to do something, not sure what I'd do, but I felt empowered.

Not long after the party, I met Lois for lunch. I was assisting her with another fundraiser she was working on for her ACTSO for Kids project. After we discussed the plans for this project, somehow we got on the subject of salaries. I was figuring how not to rock the boat but still bring up the issues I needed to at work. I complained of how I didn't want to lose my good salary of below fifty thousand. Again, she was surprised by my naïveté. She said, "You should be making at least fifty thousand *plus* with the position and responsibilities you have. I use to make that when I had little city jobs years ago." This just validated even more that I was being taken advantage of. I was about to graduate finally with my BS, but still I had no confidence that JPL would promote me to the position they promised and I deserved. *What would be the excuse for not promoting me now?* I wondered. "Ontresicia? Are you okay?"

I snapped out of my thoughts. "Yes. Sure, I'm good," I said as convincingly as I could.

"Girl what's wrong?"

"I'm just nervous. You know these people have never treated me right and now that I'm graduating, I have the years' experience required to become a Senior Buyer or Buyer Specialist. Hell I've been doing the work for that position since before the Challenger project. As a matter of fact that's how I ended up on that project."

"What do you mean?"

"After about four years of working at JPL, I had developed good negotiating skills as a buyer. Of course they didn't want to tell me I was good verbally but in a way they did by allowing me to work on high profile projects. The end-users liked the prices and quality of the products, and the vendors liked doing business with me. I had a reputation of being fair. I was executing the same types of procurements as Senior Buyers and Buyer Specialists, I just needed one of their signatures as a co-signer because they had a higher dollar signature threshold than I did.

"So you were given the responsibilities of the Senior Buyers without the pay way back in 1986 – or even before then because the Challenger fiasco happened then. But I'm sure you all had been working on it before we, the public, knew anything about it, right?"

"Let me tell you something Lois, I was so proud and excited to be a part of that project that I didn't think twice about the pay. That was my problem. The Challenger was my first huge project. I was responsible for purchasing all of the metals used to fabricate the test landing pad for the shuttle. I remember us being a bit behind schedule on the project, so we were scattering around trying to pull all of our parts together to meet the project deadline. On the day of the launching, we all met at the Von Karmon Auditorium in another building in Pasadena. When I got inside, I didn't have time to find a seat because the countdown had begun and it was too dark anyway. So I stood in awe, amazed over my part in this project and what was about to happen."

"Uh oh."

"Yeah, uh oh, because you know what happened. The shuttle had disintegrated over the Atlantic Ocean, instantly killing all seven passengers. But girl, all of a sudden, pure pandemonium broke out! The lights flipped on and everyone began shouting and scattering around frantically. I stood at the top in back of the auditorium, watching everyone running around like little mice in a maze, confused and frightened."

"So what did they do? What did they say?" Lois watched me with eyes stretched as wide as fifty cent pieces. She leaned in across the table to hear the rest of this story.

"Well, when everyone went back to the office there was a lot of talk. Still chaos. Then for the next several months, everyone involved in the project would be under investigation of some sort, and there was lots of gossip and finger pointing. Can you guess who my co-workers mainly pointed their fingers at?"

Lois jerked herself back upright in her chair and said, "Not you. I know they did not blame you." She shook her head. "No, tell me they didn't try to blame you for this." The look on my face answered her question. "Well, the bottom line is you're still there today so those were just rumors and gossip. Like you said, everyone was under investigation because of this major catastrophe. If they truly thought it was your negligence that caused this in any way, your butt would have been out of there."

"The investigation later revealed that the disintegration of the craft began after an O-ring seal in its right solid rocket booster failed at liftoff. I had not only purchased metals, but it turned out that some of the wire, cable, and O-rings I purchased were also used for the project. At least that's what we thought. Later we also found out that our O-rings were not used for the project anyway. So, it was a lot of hoopla for nothing. But like you said, if they believed I was negligent in any way, I would have been terminated without hesitation, because they definitely needed a scapegoat for that disaster. Now, getting closer to my graduation, I just wonder will this come back, now years later, to haunt me. This company has just made me paranoid."

"I think you're right. You are being paranoid but you have good reason to be. Maybe you should start talking to someone now to see if you can lock in this promotion."

"That's a good idea." We finished up our lunch and said our goodbyes. I at least had an idea of what my next step would be.

The year was winding down and everyone at JPL was in a festive, jolly mood. The plans for the Christmas potluck were underway and although I didn't celebrate Christmas I would always bring the support team gifts. The day of the party, I fixed my plate and took it back to my cubicle so that I wouldn't have to be ignored by the staff or notice the whispers or the rolling of the eyes as I entered or tried to be part of a conversation.

After I ate, I placed a gift on the desk of each support person while they were still in the conference room eating, chatting and listening to Christmas music. My gifts for the ladies were miniature scented bath gels and lotions from Vitabath. We were released to go home early after the party. As I walked to the elevator, there was a crowd of people waiting for the elevator. In the midst of the group stood Sally, one of the group support secretaries. She approached me and said, "You know Triece, I don't appreciate you giving me bath gel for Christmas, it's like you're trying to say I stink or something." She shoved the gift bag into my hand and continued, saying, "Here, you take this back because I don't want anything from you."

I stood confused with her outburst. "I'm sorry. I didn't mean it like that. I thought all women liked bath gels. I wasn't trying to say you stink. I gave it to everyone." I clutched the returned gift and turned as everyone watched me in a dead silence. As the saliva in my mouth became very thin, a warm electrical pricking sensation rushed my face while I stood there paralyzed and all choked up hoping my mask would still be intact. When the elevator door opened, most of them got on. I waited for the next elevator, appearing to not have been affected by Sally's childish tantrum.

Chapter Eight
1993 – Cal Poly Graduation

Before I knew it, a year had passed since the verdict and the riots. It was 1993 and I was graduating from Cal Poly Pomona in the summer. I couldn't believe I was actually graduating. I reflected back on my life – the relationship I had with my mom and step dad over the years, a couple of college friends, and boyfriends. Most of them, gone. That's how it had always been for me, people come, go, and come back again with some sad story. I didn't have much left in the neighborhood of personal friends, outside of work.

I thought about what Lois had told me a few months ago, that I should speak with someone at JPL to confirm my promotion as promised after I receive my B.S. degree. Things seemed even more intense than usual after that strange outburst at the Christmas party. It was time for me to put my negotiating skills to the ultimate test. A few months before graduation I called the division manager's secretary, Amber, to request an appointment to speak with the division manager, Douglas, to revisit previous discussions regarding promotion criteria. Amber gave me an appointment for that coming Friday morning. It was only Monday so I had time to prepare both physically and mentally. I went out and purchased a navy blue skirt suit, a silk blouse, and a new pair of black pumps I would wear with off black pantyhose. I wanted to look very professional and powerful.

The night before I prepared by writing a list of everything I'd need for the meeting. By then, I knew the players well and knew they wouldn't keep their promises. Some way, they'd find a way to weasel out of the agreement, or the criteria would once again be changed to deny my promotion that I had worked so hard to obtain. I must admit having a one-to-one with Douglas was intimidating, but I was ready and determined to fight for what I believed was due to me. I wasn't his equal in age, education, or experience; however, I had enough education and experience to earn this promotion and he was going to have to face me regardless of how inferior he or this company may have viewed me.

That night I couldn't sleep. I replayed possible scenes of the meeting in my mind over and over again as I tossed and turned. Finally the alarm went off at 5:00 a.m. I showered, dressed and was on the freeway to my office. When I arrived, I went to my desk and pulled a group of high dollar, complex procurements awards, performance evaluations, and paycheck stubs. I was going to be prepared. I was determined not to allow him to make me feel beneath him. My meeting was at 10:00 a.m. at the main Laboratory on Oak Grove Drive, which was about fifteen or twenty minutes away, so I left my office at 9:15 a.m. to allow for possible traffic delays.

I arrived at Douglas' office and Amber told me to have a seat; he would be with me momentarily. I sat in the reception area with my best poker face. I didn't want anyone to see how nervous I was. Amber received a call. I heard her say, "OK." She hung up and said, "He will see you now." She gestured for me to come her way, and then escorted me to a conference room down a short hall. When I entered the room I was surprised to see the black lady from the

96

Employee Relations department, Dinah Crutch, sitting in the office with Douglas. I wasn't totally alone. Dinah was the Employee Relations investigator who handled our original complaint. I felt minor relief. I shook their hands, pulled off my coat, placed it and my briefcase in the chair next to me and had a seat. I noticed they watched my every move. As I pulled my chair up to the table and looked at them, they were both glaring into my eyes with a look of authority, as to say "How dare you waltz in here for a discussion about a promotion." So there I was ready to negotiate with the Division Manager which is equivalent to a VP of Contracts and Procurement in most companies. I was brazen though, I made sure I gave them direct eye contact, and finally Dinah smiled slightly, as if to say, "That's my girl! She knew I wasn't going to let him see my tail tucked in. Dinah was very supportive and sympathetic to our concerns when we filed the complaint. There was not much she could do because of her fiduciary duty to the company. I certainly understood her position.

"Well Ontresicia, what can we do for you today?"

"I'm here to provide you with an update on my graduation date and to address the promotion you promised me upon completing my four year degree."

"I see. I hope you don't mind that I've invited Dinah Crutch. You remember her, don't you? I thought it would be a good idea to have someone to document and have some point of references. You know I don't remember all of the conversations we've had over the years."

"Sure. No problem." I glanced at Dinah then back at Douglas. "I will be graduating in a couple of months...in June...and I thought this would be a good time to have a discussion about my career path and the available opportunities for me."

"Exactly what opportunities are we discussing here today?" He asked as he stared into my eyes to see if I'd break. But I was firm as I reminded him of the promise he made that I would be eligible for a senior level position after graduation. I found myself back in the same situation, trying to make him recollect the lie he had told. "A promotion has to be earned, it is not given." He was beginning to chip away my exterior shell. He knew if he made me explain every small detail over and over again as to why I deserved a promotion, it would wear me down. But I came prepared. I leaned over, picked up my soft leather brief case, flipped open the flap, reached in and pulled out a stack of complex high dollar valued acquisitions, performance evaluations, and paycheck stubs to prove my worthiness. After reviewing my paperwork, Douglas agreed that I had definitely done the work of a Senior Buyer or Negotiator. Then he said, "Ontresicia, there's no way we can give you that big of a jump in salary. You don't meet the salary mid point of a senior level position. We will have to gradually bring your salary up. We can't justify that type of hike in salary at one time, it will never be approved."

"Aren't you the person to approve it?" I snapped.

"Of course not. It has to be approved by the compensation department. Anyway, another employee that was part of the complaint you all filed, who started a year before you, isn't going to be promoted to a senior level position either. How would it look if you are promoted to that level and she isn't? Don't you agree Dinah?"

Dinah paused before turning to Douglas and saying, "I think what Ontresicia is saying is that she was precluded from a couple of promotions in the past and with her experience, education, and performance, she deserves this promotion."

There I was again – the rules and promises had changed. I looked him square in the eyes, my jaws tightened and my teeth clenched. I felt the ticking bomb within me about to explode as I yelled, "I have taken enough off of you people. The rules just keep changing don't they? It's always been like that, right, Douglas? Just like you knew what Mr. Cotter was doing to me, and you never did anything to stop it!" Tears begin to stream down my face as I leaned in over the desk and said, "You were happy that the statue of limitations had run out by the time we filed the complaint with Employee Relations." My voice was loud and trembling, I couldn't control it. My entire face and ears were burning as the rupture within exploded. I stood up and said, "So I'm supposed to take a lesser position, after all of the work that I've done, while you people have done nothing but degrade me? This is what you have to offer me?" My mask had disappeared. I stood there raw, my anger and pain fully displayed for them to see.

Dinah looked at me astonished and disappointed, then dropped her head. Douglas' eyes dazzled with great accomplishment. I was defeated because I had lost my composure, raised my voice, and shed tears. I told them to have a good day and walked out. As I walked out, tears continued to pour from the frustration of defeat. It seemed our complaint had only benefited other blacks in the company and new hires. Dinah did such a good job at addressing our issues and applying damage control techniques that she was promoted to Director of Employee Relations by the time the complaint had been resolved. I believe that was done to emotionally remove her from the concept that we had been discriminated against. She was a Cornell graduate and should have been hired in at a much higher position than an investigator, but it wasn't until her involvement in our case that they decided to promote her – two levels higher. So, the divide and conquer started with her.

By the time I drove back to the Foothill office, Amber had already called her friend, Janiece, and given her the dirt on my meeting with Douglas and Dinah.

That night at the Menage everyone asked me questions about the meeting. One of the employees said, "Girl, I heard you went to Douglas' office and told him off." The ignorance of some of the people annoyed me. Here I was fighting for my livelihood and all they were interested in was having a gossip fest at my expense. Amber and Janiece came in together. Amber said, "Triece, Douglas looked all shaken up when he and Dinah came out of the conference room. His face was ruby red. You were talking loud. Everyone passing by could hear you." Then she and Janiece looked at each other and then back toward me, sarcastically giggling and shaking their heads. I just walked away. I was glad it was Friday so I wouldn't have to look at these people the next day.

When it was all said and done, there were fewer than twenty women in our graduating class, and maybe around seven people of African descent, which included about four from the continent of Africa. It was majoring in Business Operations Management that was intimidating to most scholars because of the emphasis on math and statistics. I thought to myself *I've been in Southern California for ten years now. Who can I invite to my graduation?* I called my mom and dad first and their initial response was "we don't think we'll be able to make it." I had an estranged relationship with them, so I thought *if they didn't come to the junior college graduation, why would they come to this one?*

When I started working at JPL in 1982, I was right out of high school. Within a year and a half, I had started college and had found myself involved with a man twelve years my senior. I think I was trying to replace the absence of a relationship with my parents with this relationship. After being involved with him for four years, I realized the relationship was and had been toxic and dangerous to my emotional and physical well-being. I wasn't prepared for such an experience. I had been sheltered from people all of my life. I held on to the relationship for so long because I didn't have a set of expectations. How could I? I had never experienced dating in high school and quite frankly, I was used to being humiliated as a child and teenager anyway. So his verbal, mental, and emotional abuse was normal to me. I had no one to talk to and no mother to tell me how to handle these issues.

I couldn't even talk to older cousins because for some reason my leaving, although it was not my decision, seemed to cause resentment between me and my family. There was so much gossip about me by some of my cousins I had been close to – even some I had practically helped raise. They were saying that I thought I was better than them because I was supposedly going to college.

So I thought again *who should I invite to this graduation from Cal Poly?* If my parents didn't want to come, it was okay, because this was for me! I invited my Uncle Wesley, Aunt Dessa, Grandpa Mac, my cousin Debra, cousin Glen, Michelle, Janet and Felicia. One Saturday morning a month before graduation, I sat out on the patio with a cup of coffee and a box of beautiful graduation announcements. Although it was short notice for the mailed invitations, it was okay because I had verbally spoken to the few people I was inviting.

Graduating excited me. It gave me hope for a brighter future. No matter how much a system, a society, or a job may try to take from you, one thing they can never take is your education. I heard this from many members of the BBA, and I believed it. I never gave up on obtaining my degree. As a matter of fact, all of the crap made me work harder for it. Education, knowledge, experience, and a good work ethic will always provide more opportunities. One thing I remember so vividly about the riots or uprising was the hopelessness and anger I saw in the eyes of many of the youths. We would like to think we are all on the same playing field but the truth is we're not. We do not all have the same opportunities in life, whether due to the environment in which we live, our family structure and support, or both.

Finally, graduation day had arrived. It took a long time, but I did it. My mom and dad drove down the night before to surprise me, and I was excited. My grandpa Mac, my parents, and most of my cousins who were here came to see me graduate. Though Glen couldn't come, it was still a beautiful day.

After the ceremony, we all went out to dinner at Luminarias restaurant. "We have reservations under Ontresicia," I said, with the biggest smile, to the maître d'.

"I see, right here, Ontresicia," he said as he made a check mark by my name on his schedule. "Is this a special occasion?"

Before I could answer, two of my family members blurted out, "Her graduation."

I laughed and said, "Yep, it's my graduation."

"Well congratulations," he said. "Come right this way." He led us out to the patio dining area. The weather was perfect – slightly warm with a soul-soothing summer breeze. It was already dusk and the lights illuminating from the San Gabriel Valley added that perfect touch. Everyone was in awe of the view. The gentleman guided us to a large table next to the railing so there were no obstacles blocking our view overlooking the mountains. "Is this okay for you, miss?"

I looked at him gleaming and said, "It's perfect." Seeing my mom and dad laughing and having a great time with me was more than I could ever ask for. We laughed and talked for hours. It was one of the best nights I had had in years.

The next day, I took my parents out for breakfast before they got on the road to go back home. We had a pleasant visit and I believe we were still on a natural high from the wonderful evening the night before.

About two weeks after graduating from Cal Poly, I met up with some friends at Menage, and I saw my first real boyfriend, Gene. I hadn't seen him since 1986. I'm glad I was looking hot, because there's nothing worse than running into an old boyfriend while looking a mess. When he saw me, he made his way through the small crowd to reach me in a hurry. After we exchanged pleasantries, he told me he was glad to see me because over the years he had time to reflect on how he treated me. He explained that he had gotten married to a schoolteacher in Atlanta and had treated her badly, used her financially, and disrespected her every chance he got. The story sounded familiar, of course. He said she pressed charges against him, and he was convicted and sent to, I think, federal prison. He said,

"When I was there, I thought about how badly I treated you, and you were just a child. I had no right to be with you, let alone take so much from you. I've always wanted to tell you how sorry I am." As I listened, I thought, *I guess prison is the one place that gives everyone an opportunity to truly reflect,* but I didn't interrupt him.

I don't know why, but his confession gave me some needed affirmation that I was and had always been a "good woman." Maybe it was because I had always felt like I was never good enough or did enough to please others – always in a state of bewilderment, wondering why I felt unworthy of love, of acceptance, of equality. Maybe that's why I pushed myself so hard to show everyone what I could accomplish and that I was a hard worker and a good person. Or, maybe I did it all to prove to myself that I was worthy of love, acceptance, and respect. As these thoughts floated through my mind, I sat on the barstool and looked up at this man who continued pouring out his heart. I remembered leaving the club that night thinking, *I really needed to hear that.*

After taking a couple of weeks off work right after graduation, I returned. On my first day back, I thought maybe with some time away I would be able to enter the building without feeling so uneasy. I was wrong. The tension was still as thick as mud.

In July 1993, the trial began for Damien "Football" Williams and Henry Watson – two of the men known as the "LA Four," charged with the beating of the white truck driver Reginald Denny – known as the "sacrificial lamb" of the riots. The other two men, Antoine Miller and Gary Williams, were not tried with Damien and Henry, and I think one of them had already pled guilty. Although I despised what the young men had done to the innocent truck driver, for some strange reason, I couldn't deny my sick attraction to Damien Williams' defense attorney, Edi Faal, for his brilliance during the trial. As I sat outside at my small patio table reading the newspaper and drinking my coffee as I did almost every Sunday, I became fascinated with the attorney's theories and arguments to defend Williams.

The attorney challenged the video evidence and attempted to portray Damien as a victim of racism and poverty. He also argued that Damien's attempt to murder Reginald Denny was stimulated by the "riot frenzy theory." What? Was he serious? With my inquisitive nature, I had to look this up to see if such a thing even existed. To my surprise I found it linked to "herd behavior," which is defined as "the manner in which individuals in a group can act together without planned direction." Really? Who would buy this?

In October, the verdict was in. Not only did the jury buy it, Damien basically got off unscathed with a fairly light sentence considering the crime. But, did that make any of us feel better? I don't think so!

The day the verdicts were read, Glen called. "Hey Triece, did you hear the verdicts?"

"Yes, I heard while I was driving home. I can't believe the jury bought that," I said while kicking my shoes off and trying to remove my jacket while balancing the phone against my ear and shoulder. I could tell Glen was down.

"Watching that whole thing on T.V. made me sick," he said. "Cousin, you know we weren't raised like that. That man didn't deserve that."

A few months after graduation, I was promoted to Contract Negotiator. However, it wasn't a huge jump in salary, nor was it the

Buyer Specialist position I had been aiming for. It sure as hell did not make up for the past mental and physical discrimination I had endured over the years, but for some reason JPL was still my security blanket. A few weeks before Christmas, my new supervisor left for vacation and asked me to finish one of his projects. He instructed me to assign all administrative duties for his project to his secretary, Sally. Yes the same Sally who threw a hissy fit the year prior because I had given her, along with the other ladies, bath gel. Sally disliked me and had been very vocal about it. Whenever I would pass her desk, she'd pretend to be choking because she hated my perfume, or she'd accuse me of looking at her strange, or something else. There was always something with Sally.

The day after my supervisor left, Sally entered my cubicle and threw Christmas cards that vendors had sent me on my desk instead of placing them in my in-basket. Some landed on the desk and others landed on the floor. I gazed up at her and said, "You need to pick those up." She looked at me as if I were the maid or nanny telling the owner what to do. She curled her lip up and gave me an evil smirk and walked away. I took in a deep breath and thought *I really don't feel like dealing with this drama today*. The nonsense had escalated to a whole new level. I asked myself over and over, *why am I still here?*

About a half hour later, I walked to her desk and placed an assignment in her in-basket and said "I need this expedited," which meant I needed the work completed and given back to me the same day. There was no need for discussion so I returned to my desk. I called a vendor and while on the phone, Sally entered my cubicle again and began yelling, "I don't work for you, Triece, you need to give your work to your own secretary."

I stopped writing and placed my hand over the phone to prevent the vendor from hearing her and said, "This work is for your boss and he instructed me to give you the assignments for that project, I'll talk to you after I finish this call." I gestured for her to go away. Instead, I think she lost her mind because this woman grabbed my arm and begin hitting me, although not hard, but still hitting me. I dropped the phone and stood up thinking that would remind her that she wasn't dealing with a child, but she wouldn't let go of my arm. It took all of my strength not to beat her down. With the look of death in my eyes and through clenched teeth, I said in a low growl, "You better get your mothafuckin' hands off of me." I jerked away as I pushed her away from me at the same time. She ran out as if I had done something awful to her. She went to the new black group supervisor, and I could only imagine what she told him.

Eventually, the supervisor called me into his office and questioned me about what happened. I told him everything and they pretty much did nothing. Once again, I filed a complaint with the Employee Relations department, and Sally eventually left, due to "stress". But I remained, hanging in there and taking everything that came my way. I felt I deserved to be there after all I had been through and no one was going to make me leave.

Chapter Nine
The Love of Money –
The Root of All Evil

I n the beginning of 1993, everything was back to business as usual for the community, but for Glen it was the beginning of the civil trial and more disappointments. Two of the officers that had beaten him, Koon and Powell, were convicted of violating Glen's civil rights. The other two, Wind and Briseno, were found not guilty. Trials continued for Glen's suit against the city of Los Angeles and the officers.

Meanwhile, I continued working at JPL, as I harbored ill feelings for what this company had done to me emotionally and physically. I hadn't shared, in depth, with any family members what I was going through at JPL. I just worked hard and hoped it would all work out for me in the end.

One Wednesday late in the summer, I left work early and went to the Glendale Galleria mall to do some shopping. I hadn't showered myself with any gifts lately, and boy did I deserve some. As I entered the narrow, dark parking structure and began my task of finding a parking spot while traveling around and around the structure, I remembered I had decided never to enter from Central St. again. The parking maze usually stressed me out before I could reach any sales.

This time though, I was lucky that someone pulled out right by the JCPenney's door.

As I walked through the mall, dipping into stores looking for a nice outfit to perk my spirits up, I hoped I wouldn't run into anyone. I had become accustomed to the usual "Girl, how are you doing? Is your cousin staying out of trouble?" It never failed somehow that any conversation I had with friends would turn to Glen. I just wanted a peaceful shopping day. But, Glen had been in the news again a couple of weeks ago. He had crashed into a wall near a downtown Los Angeles nightclub. His blood alcohol level was over the legal limits again. Weeks prior to this incident, Koon and Powell had been sentenced to only thirty months in a federal correctional camp. Civil groups complained that the sentence did not fit the crime.

I finally found the perfect gray suit in a very sleek, professional style. The skirt was straight with two slits in the back, and it was made of light wool so I could wear it year round. I found a deep burgundy blouse and now all I needed were the shoes to complete the outfit. On my way to the car I stopped to get a coke and a warm chocolate chip cookie from Mrs. Fields.

While in the dressing rooms, I noticed my eyebrows were a little raggedy so I decided to go see Chuck to get my eyebrows arched. It was Wednesday, so I figured there wouldn't be too many people in the shop. I veered off of the 210 to Lake Ave. and peeked into the shop as I drove past. It didn't look like anyone was there. I strutted to the door and swung it open with a huge smile on my face.

"Hey Chuck, how are you?"

"Hey Ontresicia. Haven't seen you in a while girl. What's going on?"

Before I could answer, my friend Tyrone came from the back. "Nothing is going on. Just doing a little shopping and decided I really needed you to do your magic on these eyebrows. Do I need to wait?" I said, looking at Tyrone. "Hi Tyrone." I gave him a hug.

"Hey Ontresicia. How's everything going?"

Chuck said, "No I'm finished with that guy." Shooing Tyrone with his hands, he said, "Come on over here and sit down."

"Hey Ontresicia, we haven't seen you in a bit," Tyrone said very cheerfully.

"I know. I've been really busy at work." I relaxed and laid my head back as Chuck began smoothing the warm wax on my brows. I was in a place where I could let my guard down and maybe for once talk about something other than Glen. Chuck pressed the cloth over one brow then snatched it off quickly, leaving me feeling that tingling sensation of pain and pleasure. As he began smoothing the wax on the other brow, Chuck said, "So Ontresicia, what cha brother, I mean…" with a little snicker, "…your cousin been into lately?" They both laughed as he continued. "You tell Rodney he needs to get somewhere and sit down and be still." Then he snatched the second strip from my eyebrows. All I felt was pain.

The black community had begun to change their opinions of Glen. He was getting into a lot of mischief and was making the news constantly. They'd broadcast things about his life that they would not take the time to report about someone else who may have done the same things. It seemed like the goal of the media was to prove how reckless he was. He was being tried by the media and each time he misbehaved, the settlement purse of the civil trial decreased. Some of the same people who helped out in 1991 with advice and direction, like my friends Tyrone and Chuck, were now making jokes about him. My first impulse was to jump up and defend him as I usually did; but seeing Tyrone, a man I admired and respected for so long, laugh at the comments just took the fight out of me. I just played it off by saying, "You know Glen." I paid for my service without any more conversation and left.

Later that week, I was sitting in my bed reading some magazine article when the phone rang. I checked the caller ID. It was Johnnie. I grabbed the phone in excitement since I hadn't spoken to him for a while.

"Hello Ontresicia, how are you doing?" he said in his usual hurried tone.

"I'm fine. How have you been doing?"

"I'm fine. Look, the reason I'm calling is….um, you need to do something." Johnnie was not one for small talk. He was direct and to the point. "You know, Rodney is really messing things up. You need to talk to him. Milton will be lucky if he can settle this case for a million dollars at this point. This is a crucial time; so Rodney really needs to behave himself."

"OK Johnnie. I'll talk to him." That was the second to the last conversation I had with Johnnie. I had grown attached to his seemingly personal concern and advice. Prior to that call, from time to time, he would contact me to see if I was doing okay, and his conduct was always professional but fatherly at the same time. But even he became disappointed in Glen – something I thought with all the excitement and interest around Glen could never happen.

The following week, I drove to Glen's house in Altadena – hoping everything was peaceful and quiet. I needed him to be focused on what I had to tell him. I knocked on the door several times before he answered.

"Hey Cous," he said as he flung the door open for me to come in.

"Hey Glen. What's going on? Are you alright?" I could tell something was bothering him, but I needed to get my words in first before he started in on something else. I followed him to the kitchen and sat at the barstool. He was making one of his health concoctions with a bunch of vegetables. It didn't look good but it certainly looked healthy.

"What's up Cous?" he said cheerfully but his eyes told a different story.

"Not too much. I just wanted to come by and see how you were doing and give you a message from Johnnie."

"I don't need to hear no shit from or about no lawyers today. I'm sick of all those niggas. All of them ain't nothing but a bunch of big time gangstas."

I thought, *uh oh, what happened now*? "What's wrong Glen? What happened?" I asked.

"Cous, I don't even want to talk about them." He finished blending the veggies and poured the juice in a tall glass. "You want some of this?"

I cringed. "No." Later he confided in me that Grimes was trying to change something around in the contract but I never understood exactly what went wrong. He was upset with all lawyers at that point. He had put personal trust in each of them: Steve, his mom, and the legal crew, then Grimes and his wife, Eloise, and the slew of attorneys Grimes hired as experts and researchers. Star Jones was even part of the legal crew. I had never heard of her working in

California until Glen's case. Glen and his friend and assistant, Johnny Kelley, loved Star. They'd talk about her all the time. They told me about some of their fun experiences with her, like getting her to order a couple of hundred dollars worth of cheeseburgers in her hotel suite so they could laugh and joke around to blanket all the madness during the trial. I never met Star, but she captivated them, and she hadn't really become a celebrity yet – at least not in Cali.

Glen had become attached to these people, like they were family. He socialized with them. Glen didn't just see him as his attorney, but he loved Milton like a father figure. Milton and Eloise made him feel like he was one of their children and no matter what, they'd always have his back and his best interest in mind. I knew this because of how he would speak of them. It wasn't just a professional relation-ship.

Milton kept Glen preoccupied by hiring Judy Sampson to tutor him. From my observation, based on Glen's attitude and things he'd told me, Milton was different from Steve. He was molding Glen to become a better person – or at least trying to. Milton was definitely in control of things. Glen was on a strict regimen. He would get dressed up and he and Johnny would go to Orange County for his tutoring. He'd also keep an eye on what was going on with the case. Although I was busy with work, from my observation, Grimes hired a bunch of people whose jobs were to manage Glen until the civil trial was over, and that's exactly what they tried to do. For a while it worked; but trouble seemed to always find Glen. Or Glen found trouble.

Before the civil trial ended, things between Milton and Glen had gotten worse due to this disagreement about the signed contract that Milton claimed was superseded by a verbal agreement that Glen had no recollection of. All I can say is that, it's not my story to tell, but it's a story all by itself.

Glen and I discussed the problems he was having, and he became very emotional, paranoid, and stressed. I could see the anger and confusion in his eyes as he explained how Milton betrayed him. Once again, I turned to Johnnie for help. I called him under the assumption that maybe he would be willing to assist us. I wasn't aware of the camaraderie the black attorneys had for one another. Johnnie returned my phone call. I told him, "Milton and Glen had a conflict and Glen needs some help. I was wondering if you could finish the case?"

"Absolutely not!" he snapped. It was a painful rejection. He continued saying, "First of all, with all the bad publicity, with the wrong jury, Rodney may not be awarded compensatory damages." There were other awards he explained but I can't remember. Maybe punitive, attorney fees, and something else. I think there were three or four in total. "And there may not be enough of an award to split amongst all of the attorneys who had touched the case." Looking back, Johnnie was right. Why would he come into this mess at this point? Glen was "shit out of luck". He would have to stick it out with Grimes, no matter how painful it was.

Meanwhile, Glen was becoming very distant from his immediate family. Aunt Dessa called me one day and asked if I would go to check on Glen from time to time. She felt he was only depending on his wife's family and she wanted him to know we were here for him as well. So I did as she asked and began stopping by the house to check on Glen more frequently. He was an emotional wreck. His moods and personality seemed to swing every couple of minutes or so. The severed friendship between him and Milton was very painful for him. I asked his friend Johnny, "What do you think is causing his mood swings?" I thought he'd know because he was around Glen the most. He said, "He's been like this since he and Milton fell out."

One Saturday, as I was visiting Glen, he was drinking pureed bell peppers (he was on a real health kick back then) and he looked at me and said, "Your eyes are red, you need to drink some of this too." I was stressed. I had eaten all the crowns off the back of my teeth and had developed a TMJ disorder – chronic inflammation of my temporomandibular joint – from grinding my teeth at night according to my dentist. I wasn't getting very much sleep either. My life was getting worse at JPL, and I wanted out. I finally shared my story in detail about JPL with Glen. He said, "Cous, I know a slew of attorneys, you need to fight them. I didn't know they were doing that kinda shit to you. Man!" I guess I could have spoken to Johnnie over the years, but I was ashamed to tell him. If I told him all of the crap I was going through, his opinion of me being a strong, confident professional woman would have changed. I would never take that chance. Besides, his calls were to help Glen. Glen wanted me to fight them. He said, "I can't tell you what to do, but that's what I'd do." He then got on his treadmill and began running.

As I sat there watching him, I finally really understood what Lois Gammel had been trying to tell me. I had been a victim of racial and sexual discrimination! I was finally old enough to understand that someone needed to be held accountable for the way I felt. It took my own experience coupled with Glen's to understand fully what I had gone through over the years. The humiliation and embarrassment was greater in hindsight, but I guess that's because when one part of the abuse stopped, another type began. It was like an abusive, toxic relationship with a man and I had held on to it like it was *my* man.

Glen jumped off the treadmill and moved on to the sky machine. He did circuit training all the time. It was his way of dealing with his stress. Although the civil trial had ended, Glen was awarded damages from the city of Los Angeles, but nothing from the civil suit against the officers. At the end of his workout, he told me that he wanted me to talk to one of the jurors from his civil case who also worked at JPL and had gone through some similar things. Glen told me she was nice and that she and her husband had invited him, along with Johnny over for a lobster dinner. He said that she really cooked well and that they were just good people. We hung out for a while talking, and I decided I would take his advice and talk to his friend.

That next week, while at work, Roger told me he was concerned about me. "Although I have a fiduciary responsibility to JPL, you are my friend and I'm worried about your well being. You've been through a lot here. Most people would have sued for what you've gone through over the years." He continued to explain that Sally, the secretary who had grabbed me, had been quietly forced out of her position – not gone on stress leave as we were told. Roger said she was management's favorite and they were not happy that they could not save her job. He explained that my job would eventually be in jeopardy. It was only a matter of time before they would build some bogus case against me to get me out. He encouraged me to go to a JPL doctor and tell them everything so that they could take me out of work for stress in order to buy myself some time. I was afraid to do that, but at this point I was ready to go; so I saw this as my way out.

That was the best thing I did for myself. I finally walked out on what I thought was my dream job.

I had a lot of time on my hands when I went out on stress leave. Glen and I really got a chance to bond even more. We were both stressed, but for some reason we had this way of balancing one another. He would try to look over me and protect me, and I would try to do the same for him. He was also intrigued with the fact that I had earned my degree – an accomplishment no other cousin of ours had achieved. I could tell he was proud of me, although he didn't come to my graduation.

Around this time, Glen didn't trust his wife, Crystal, or Johnny Kelley. One day during one of my visits, Glen was trying to organize his papers. Whenever Glen was stressed, he would pull out all of those freakin' contracts, trying to find the agreement that Grimes kept talking about and no one had a copy of; and he'd make the biggest mess. I asked him if he wanted me to help him get his files together. He said, "Yeah, I need some help." So at least once a week I would go over to help him put his papers in order.

The 3.8 million dollar settlement from the civil trial was distributed in October 1994 to Steve Lerman's office. Yes, Glen went back to Steve, and of course, that would be a new contract. At this point, Steve had been hired to receive and distribute monies. The bloodbath had begun.

To this day in my life, I have never seen anything remotely similar to what I saw happening to my cousin. In short, Lerman and Grimes entered into contractual agreements with Glen to receive a smaller percentage than they would have normally agreed to. Although Glen didn't have a formal education, and was considered, in every sense of the word, illiterate, prior to Judy's tutoring sessions, he negotiated some very good deals for himself. Of course, the case had the highest profile of any racially motivated case since the '50s and '60s – the days of the Birmingham church bombings and Emmett Till. Most attorneys wanted a piece of the case, just for the historical part of it. I guess they knew they'd find a way to take his money after everything was over.

Finally, Steve distributed a portion of the award to Glen, but the largest amount remained at his office in an escrow account since attorney fees remained in dispute. Everyone wanted money: the wife (with whom he was going through an ugly divorce), the ex-wife (his baby's mother), the ex-girlfriends, the family members, and the list went on. There was a lot of pulling and tugging from everyone. Friends came out of the woodwork to make a claim. Everyone who passed through had advice for Glen as to what he should be doing with his money.

Although Glen had been awarded the big settlement, he was still having legal issues. The money seemed to make everything worse. He hadn't worked for years. He couldn't. He fought legal battles for a long time after he was out of the public's eye (well, I guess he's never really been out of the public's eye.) It was an ugly, hurtful, painful sight to watch. They tore him down like a pride of lions ravenously attacking a lonely hyena, exhausted and run-down in the middle of a savannah, consumed by the lions and left for the vultures and maggots. He was exhausted and untrusting of everyone; and most of the time he was somewhat disoriented, babbling, blundering and repeating the same words over and over again. "I can't find it. I can't find no fuckin' second contract." as he continued to rack his brain, trying to remember all of the conversations he had with Milton.

Black leaders had become embarrassed of him. He hadn't lived up to the image they expected of him. They wanted him to make all sorts of speaking engagements and stay out of trouble. They wanted him to be like a Dr. King! Well, Glen wasn't Dr. King. He wasn't anything like Dr. King.

He worked tirelessly with Judy Sampson to improve his grammar, reading, and speaking skills. He'd rise early every morning to review speeches and scripts. Soon he had become a developed speaker – someone who could hold an intelligent conversation and converse with people in a manner the black leaders were accustomed to. People began to love him again, like they did after the beating. He was charming, charismatic and more than easy on the eyes. Women couldn't get enough of him, and some men used their women to get next to him. They were looking for his weak, vulnerable spot.

There was this girl, I'll call her Diane, who Glen liked a lot. She left her kids with her mom to move in with him. Glen sent her to school. She lived there rent-free. She ate freely, and Glen gave her money whenever she needed it. Eventually, Glen found out she had a boyfriend and they were playing him the whole time. The boyfriend got mad when he saw his girl was getting too close to Glen and told him what they had been plotting.

I tried my best to keep these no-good people away from him, but Glen was and still is his own person. He was so friendly towards everybody, that he didn't realize how naïve he was being. He just accepted people for what and who they said they were.

One time he met some local skinheads, hung out with them for a few months, and then went up to Tahoe with them. Yes, that's right, skinheads. He had a "life threatening experience". That's all he would say when he returned.

Working hard to be something he obviously was not, being used by women and men, still suffering personal attacks from the community, and of course me with my high expectations pushing him proved to be a combustible mixture. This was what ignited his return to his old behavior and his substance abuse.

The conflict over money continued. Lerman wanted to serve as his money manager, and Grimes wanted the entire portion that was being held, which was more than the portion Glen himself had received. Soon, after the money had been distributed to Lerman's office, I met some of the players from Grimes' team. John Burris was one of them. I was at Glen's house one evening when he called. He begged me to ask Glen to release some money to him because his daughter was very ill and in the hospital fighting for her life. My heart went out to him. We talked for a long time. When Glen came home that evening, I told him what happened. Glen said, "Cousin, I don't have the money. Steve is holding it. You know that." He said, "Grimes hired him," speaking of John Burris, "and the rest of those attorneys, and he's supposed to pay them." I didn't know the ins and outs of Glen's contract with Grimes; and for whatever reason, Milton hadn't given Glen a copy of all of the supposedly new verbal agreement that superseded the original written agreement. I knew that from organizing Glen's paperwork.

The next day, Glen and I went to Steve's office to tell him about the phone call from John Burris. Steve explained to us that if he cut a check for John, it might imply that Glen hired John and the other attorneys on Milton's crew, as opposed to Milton hiring them. Steve said he'd have to research the matter to make sure it wouldn't jeopardize Glen's chance of receiving the rest of the award.

Not long after the John Burris situation, Judy Sampson, Glen's tutor, called. Glen hadn't been accepting calls from anyone on Milton's crew and she was no different. He didn't trust her either. I hadn't met her in person, but I remembered Glen and Johnny Kelley going to Orange County to meet with her routinely. On the phone, I could tell she too was sincere. She told me to tell Glen that she and Dan are his friends, and that she loves him and only wants the best for him. She began to cry and continued saying "just tell Glen I don't have anything to do with Milton and his mess! In fact, tell Glen he doesn't have to pay Milton on behalf of me, because what I did was from the heart, and I never submitted a bill to Milton."

When I saw Glen, I told him what Judy said, but he didn't buy it. He felt Milton had put her up to it. I believed her. I could hear the pain in her voice. It was the same pain I heard in John Burris' voice, but Judy was not asking for money.

On another occasion, around May or June of 1995, Judy called again asking for Glen, who was out at an event with his kids that day. I gave her the address to where he was. She found Glen, who was still vulnerable with pain from Milton's deceit, but somehow Judy managed to show her sincerity and vulnerability. They made up and Judy became very close to Glen again. No matter what the problem was, I could always count on Judy to come through for Glen. Whenever she came around, I could see she was very torn over her working relationship with Milton and personal friendship with

Glen. She and I talked about it often and she tried desperately to convey to me that she'd never do anything to hurt Glen. I appreciated that.

In the summer of 1995, Glen was going through vicious marital problems, and he said he had to get away, so he went to Northern California for a while. He'd come back often to check on his family. During one of his visits to Southern California, he and his then wife, Crystal, had an altercation and she was hurt. I wasn't there so I don't know what really happened, but I was told that they got into a heated argument while Glen was driving and she jumped out of the "moving" car and hit her head on the cement.

We figured charges would be filed, so I helped him look for an attorney. I remembered the attorney, Edi Faal, who defended Damien "Football" Williams and seemed to be on top of his game. We called him but he didn't want the case. He said we needed a woman to represent Glen.

He gave us a number to an attorney in the Inland Empire, but she didn't want the case either. So I told Glen to call Edi back to see if he'd at least meet with him. He heard Glen out, checked the system, and said no charges had even been filed. Either the next day or two, a District Attorney in Alhambra, named Donna, filed charges against Glen. Glen called Edi back, who agreed to meet with Glen and to represent him; but it was a year before the case went to trial.

While Glen and I were driving back to Altadena, we stopped at a store right off of Fair Oaks in Pasadena. Glen went inside, but I remained in the car. My heart dropped when I spotted my ex-boyfriend, Richard. I had dated him after Gene. I thought Gene was bad but this idiot was psycho. As soon as I realized it, I dumped him.

But some people can't let go. That was Richard. After I had broken up with him, he came to my job after work on a Friday and said he needed to talk to me. He offered to drive me home, because I was still taking the bus back then. I refused at first but then agreed. Instead, he took me to his apartment, claiming he needed to get something. After I realized he had no intentions of taking me home. I told him I was leaving. He blocked the door. I said a few choice words to him, which must have unleashed the demon living within because he rammed back and socked me and began punching me. I started fighting for my life. We were in his apartment fighting like a couple of boxers in a ring. We fought so much and so hard we both were tired but he got the best of me. He held me hostage. Two days passed, and once he went to work, I escaped. I went to the police to file charges. They said I didn't have any bruises so there was nothing they could do. I had swelling in my head and some bruises that were not visible. I guess years of living with a boxer paid off, I bobbed and weaved protecting my face but I was in serious pain from the body shots.

I went to Glen and asked him to beat the guy up for me because I was damned if I was going to let him get a way with it. Glen refused saying, "You're just going to go back to him and I would be in more trouble." I promised Glen I would never go back to Richard. After that, I was enraged, so I went to my uncle Wesley and told him what Richard had done to me. He was furious. We went to Richard's apartment, but he wasn't there. We went to his mother's place, but he wasn't there either. We told her what he had done and that we were looking for him. She saw death in my uncle's eyes so I'm sure she warned her son. That was years ago. I never saw him again until that day in Pasadena. Richard looked at me with a cunning smile, but didn't say a word. I stared back as he continued walking until he disappeared from my view.

Glen finally returned. I told him I had seen Richard. "Did he say anything to you?" he asked. I told him he hadn't and we never spoke of Richard again.

Towards the end of the year, there was a knock at my door. It was Glen and a female friend. Glen had been up north for a while but was back in town and wanted to know if I had enough room for him to stay with me. He explained what had been going on with him and his wife. They were separated. I explained to Glen that I had been out of work for almost a year. I thought I was feeling better, but the doctors weren't sure after my last assessment if I should return to work or apply for long term disability. Glen said, "Don't worry Cous. You don't have to go back there. We can become roommates and you can find something else to do, like go to law school. That's what you really wanted to do." That was one of my adult dreams. I had begun prepping for the LSAT shortly after receiving my B.S. "Or you can keep helping me with all of my paperwork and preparing to fight these attorneys until you figure out what you want to do," Glen continued.

Although I had told the doctors I was feeling better, the reality was, every time I thought about going back to JPL, my body tensed up again. So I told Glen, "If we get a larger space we could become roommates." He agreed and we moved into a four bedroom home in Upland, with the police department in the building right behind our backyard. This later proved to be a very unfortunate thing for Glen.

Glen wanted to help me as much as I wanted to continue helping him. We needed and took care of one another. Glen enrolled us into a tennis class, in addition to the weights and workout equipment in the house. He also told me to enroll in a gym. In a very short time my body was in tiptop condition, but the lingering demons of JPL still possessed my mind. Glen tried to prepare me mentally and physical-ly for the legal battles we would face. Another blood bath began.

Chapter Ten
Straight Alta-Pazz Record Label

F riends and family were advising Glen about what he should do with the partial award he had received so far. Everyone contributed great ideas for how he should invest this money. However, I asked him, "What is your dream? Your passion? Glen, you need to do what's going to make you happy."

In 1995, Tupac filled the air with his lyrics from "Me Against the World," "Dear Momma," and "All Eyez on Me." There was so much pain in his lyrics, which represented so many young blacks who had been born during the mass addiction of the rock cocaine era or had been raised during the early era of the 1970s. In those times, people rebelled by freeing themselves with drugs as they attempted to fight or escape the woes of society while their children suffered and watched. His melodies were hard, yet sensitive, and his big, droopy, soft eyes allowed you to see into his soul and feel his heart at the same time. Through all of his anger, the world saw his crying eyes – just like I saw in Glen's.

In the mid-90s, there was so much controversy across the nation about gangs, the riot aftermath, Tupac and Biggie's assassination, the OJ trial, and the continued police brutality across the country.

"I really want to start my own record label. I want to pull rap artists together from all over and have them come together to work on a project."

This is when Glen came up with the notion that he would prove to the world that he could bring together artists of all sets and create a project that would be a true reflection of our community without violence. He asked me to help him with this project, and of course, I agreed. I believed in him and I believed in this project. It was what our community needed.

C. Delores Tucker, a U.S. politician and civil rights activist best known for her participation in the Civil Rights Movement and stance against gangsta rap music, had been in the limelight constantly protesting rap songs. I have to admit, I felt the lyrics of some rappers dissed black women and assisted in inciting the disrespect that we still get today; so when this project came up, I thought it would be a way to get more positive lyrics out there – not only about our community, but also in an effort to bring the generations together and create a more positive environment for the hard-working woman.

For the first year, we learned everything we could about the music business and began a major hunt for new artists to sign to the label, which we named Straight Alta-Pazz Records, after the Pasadena-Altadena area where he grew up. However, we had no luck.

Meanwhile, we continued to fight the legal battles together. We won some and lost some. It depleted both of us, but I was determined to muster up enough strength to build Glen back up and focus on what he wanted to do – build his record company, his new found passion. I shifted into overdrive and began working this music project vigorously.

We had been invited to Johnnie Cochran's Christmas party that year. It was a nice break from working so hard to find artists and I was looking forward to it. It was a huge event and I was just so happy for us to have been invited. I had been out shopping. The day prior to the party, I had bought a little number from Barneys, and had gone out to get my hair whipped. When I returned home, I received a call from someone in Johnnie's office asking us not to attend the party. I thought, of course, that this was a mistake. I asked the gentleman if he had spoken to Johnnie. He said he had and that Johnnie was the one who had asked him to call. He explained that Milton Grimes would be there and he was a personal friend of Johnnie's. He didn't want anyone to feel uncomfortable.

When I told Glen, his comment was, "I don't give a shit. Fuck them. I didn't want to go to their stupid party anyway. We'll have our own Christmas party." I, on the other hand, was disappointed and felt totally humiliated; but for the first time in my life, we celebrated Christmas in our home. We bought a huge tree. I cooked all of the traditional foods, and we invited friends and family over to celebrate. The celebration got a little crazy. Glen decided he would invite all of his kids, ex-girlfriends, ex-wives, and baby-mommas. All of us, in one house at the same time, was pure pandemonium; but he seemed to have enjoyed himself.

Unfortunately (or maybe it was fortunate for us), Glen was still getting into some problems. Due to another run-in with the law, he was scheduled to perform community service, during which time he met Pappoose, one-half of a Los Angeles-based rap duo called Stranded. He and Glen talked about Glen's project and Papoose informed him that he and his best friend Buzz rapped and had a demo tape.

128

Glen came home all excited one day. "Hey Cous. Listen to this!" He slid the CD into the stereo and turned the volume up. Both of us began rocking to the beat. When the song finished, he said, "What you think about them?"

"I think they're pretty good. Do you like them?"

"Yeah, I think they're good."

"But can they rap tongue twist runs?" I didn't know the rap lingo but I knew what was popular and we needed some rappers with all the skills.

"I'll call Papoose and find out, but I think these are the guys I wanna sign."

"OK. I'll call Desiree to get the papers drawn up." Desiree Gordy was the entertainment lawyer we met through Mack 10, the first cousin of Glen's first wife, Dee Dee. After Glen spoke to Pappoose and found out that Buzz was very skilled in rapping in tongue twisters, Glen was ready to sign. But then we found out that Pappoose was still under contract with Death Row Records – a minor glitch in our plans. However, Desiree investigated and found that Pappoose was no longer bound to his contract due to a clause about a time frame which had expired. I told her to double check because we didn't want any problems with Death Row Records. Desiree drew up the contract and we signed the group to Straight Alta-Pazz. This was our first project together – The Stranded Project.

I needed people in the business to work with me so that I could start planning this project. I needed consultants, promoters, producers, and engineers just to assist me in rolling it out. Glen's friend, Brian Baccus, was a promoter. He said, "I can't help you in the part that you need, but I can hook you up with John and Billy Valentine."

They were the artists who had a hit record called "Money's Too Tight To Mention", that was later re-made by Simply Red who took it global. The rest is history. He's been getting paid ever since. After meeting with John, he said he could help us.

"I need to know the phases of developing a music project," I told him.

"My wife, Carolyn, works for Capitol Records and could help you get to the places and people you need," John said. "I also have a friend, Leo Ralph, a promoter who worked with Andre Harrell and Russell Simmons. I'll talk to him to help kick things off." Leo also had a lot of contacts for producers so he introduced us to many of the producers in LA and Long Beach, and he hooked us up with a promoter and stage manager, Blair Mitchell.

We worked hard so that the CD would be released no later than the summer of 1998. Glen was on his way, and the pursuit revived and rejuvenated him to a whole new level of confidence and pride. He wanted his music to speak to the police brutality issues, but at the same time, speak against negativity in general. He wanted to send positive messages to the community – not just promote rap for the sake of rapping.

The more the word got out, the more beat makers and producers wanted to get involved. A lot of them were straight hustlers. Some were angry and felt Glen owed them something. I didn't understand. Maybe they felt I should've paid more for their beats, I don't know. One of the beat makers said, "We rode for Rodney, we burnt this mothafucka down for Rodney, and what kinda fuckin' gratitude has he sho'd us? Talkin' bout 'can we all fuckin' get along'…kinda shit is that?" I was shocked and a bit frightened. I thought most people took this comment as a gesture to stop the violence, but hearing this beat maker mock those words reminded me of how one of my friends had joked about it saying, "Can we all get along? What is that supposed to mean to us?" What did people want from him? Names of famous rappers were thrown around on the streets as contributors to the L.A. burning (names I will never reveal, secrets I'm taking to my grave).

Everyone gave me information I needed to pull the project together and make it successful. Glen really wanted to bring two sets together – Blue and Red, East and West – to show this world that we could work together in harmony. Most of the people we were introduced to also wanted to see it succeed.

Desiree taught me how to put the contracts together for buying or leasing music. Once we finalized the recording, Leo suggested that we have a release party. I thought it was a little too soon and Desiree agreed. But Leo insisted, "I have some other artists that can make it look good." Glen and I agreed that this was out of our league. We didn't know the protocol. And although others may have voiced their opinion that the release party was a tad premature, they couldn't mount a convincing argument since Leo was the expert.

Brian, the party promoter, made arrangements at some $25,000 party hall in West LA. I thought it was way too expensive, but again, I didn't stop and say, "No." Neither did Glen. However, for that kind of money, I insisted on getting the executives and distribution people to be there. The people we needed to impress would have to be there.

Glen and Brian had some words over something right before we paid the deposit for this big release party, but we were still moving forward, so I gave Brian the deposit money, which was half of the $25,000. This was going to happen. Something we had worked hard for. Something Glen could hold his head up high for. He could be known for something other than the face of the L.A. riots.

Glen and I helped street promoters pass out flyers on Hollywood and Vine for the release party. We were so excited. I asked Brian if he had it advertised on the radio. He tried to get time slots for radio but he didn't. He and Glen got into a huge argument again and Brian silently turned and walked out. We hadn't heard from Brian the day of the event, but I went in to pay the remaining balance. The twenty-five thousand was only to rent the venue. Additional costs for food and drinks were astronomical, but first impressions were vital in this business.

The night of the party, we had bottles of Cristal champagne at every VIP table. For all guests, we had Cognac and other expensive drinks, roast beef, roasted turkey, and vegetables trays. It was like a high-end wedding reception.

I walked in, looking all glamorous – every five feet four inches of me. My hair was in a French roll, my make up was flawless, and my silky sexy dress draped low in the back while hugging my sleek body to perfection. This was an elaborate event with radio and media coverage.

However, we noticed there weren't many people coming into the venue. I was walking around just dumbfounded, wondering why there were hardly any people inside. Then one of the security guards came up to me to tell me that Brian was outside, redirecting people to go to another event he was having and had begun promoting for the same night to sabotage our release party. All to get back at Glen. He sent most of the people coming to our party to the Hollywood Athletic Club on Sunset so no one would go to Glen's party.

I couldn't believe what was happening. There were several people we considered VIP and would, of course, have free admission in addition to regular party goers who knew there would be a charge for this event. A lady came in with several guests. She was on the VIP list, but her guests were not. I told her the other guests would need to pay. She had a hissy fit and boasted that she was the mother of a certain music producer. At that point, I didn't care or I was just not thinking. All I could see were dollar signs being flushed down the toilet. Anyway, she left; and her son, a music producer who I had spoken to in the past and wanted to have connections with, never spoke to me again.

To make matters even worse, some of our family members came in from Sacramento. Cousin Cynthia, Gerry Ann and a friend witnessed the hugely failed release party. The performers were great, but the place was empty. My cousin, Cynthia, told people that Rodney didn't make any money because she saw me running down the stairs with the cash register. This is when the rumors began. I was actually running down the stairs yelling and cussing out Brian as a few media people watched. Thank God they were there to enjoy the party and not report on it. But, people see what they want to see.

We made no money, but everybody had to get paid, from the stage manager to promoters to security. John Valentine had been out of town while this big release party was being planned; and when he found out, he said, "You should have never had a release party this soon. You weren't ready. That should not have been done."

After it was all said and done, after I had lost my personally-invested fifteen thousand dollars and even more Glen had put up, it turned out to be a well over thirty-five thousand dollar lesson.

I told Glen, "We need to stop this project right now before we lose anymore money. I don't think we should move forward."

"Well I want to move forward. If you don't do it, I'll find somebody else to do it." I thought to myself, I need to stay to help protect him from these vultures and to try to recoup some of my own money. I told him I would continue working with him on the project, but that I was more determined than ever to make it happen.

The music had already been mastered. He wanted a curse-free project, but he had a bunch of people who would get in his head, telling him, "It wasn't hot enough." People would tell him that "it would be hot if Triece would not have been at every session putting all of these constraints on us". But, I was only enforcing what Glen wanted.

We also wanted a Southern flair, which is why we picked a song from a guy named Lamar. It was really hot! Everybody in the camp loved the beat. The producer, Clay, basically told me we couldn't buy the music because it had been promised to TLC. I told Clay, "Look, everybody is willing to sell for a negotiated price." Then I asked, "Did TLC give you a down payment on the beat?"

"Not yet."

"Well then you have a decision to make. Either you can get paid now, or you can wait for them, and they may not even buy it. So what's it gonna be?" By then I had learned how hard it was for producers to sell beats, and in this game, like any other game, money talked. We went back and forth negotiating, and I finally broke him.

I was trying to negotiate a regional distribution deals for this project to keep it in the western region. The plan was to use the one stop shops, which were like huge music supermarkets where the mom-

and-pop record stores bought their music to sell. The major stores like Blockbuster and Wherehouse Records had their music delivered to them via distribution companies.

Things started off slowly and rough, but we stuck it out. We were beginning to get noticed by influential people in the industry. Things were looking up as we kept our ambitions high.

Chapter Eleven
A Man's World

Monts into this project, I was feeling a lot of stress, but it was a fun stress. As I was driving to the studio one day, I was listening to KACE. The song "It's A Man's World" by James Brown came on the oldies station. Sitting in my car hearing that song made me think of how true that statement was in my life right then. The record business was not used to women making decisions, purchasing music, and negotiating contracts. I was very quick to discover that the rap industry, in particular, was a man's world, and I had no place in it. Some of the artists and producers resented that I was the one out there representing the label. They wanted to see Glen, but Glen didn't really want to deal with the business aspect; he wanted to be the creator and the promoter. Most of the naysayers told me I could never pull it off. What they didn't know was what I had already been through. If I knew nothing else, I knew business and I had worked with the best and the worst. One thing about surviving discrimination, abuse, and hard times is that it builds you up, makes you strong, and provides you with another layer of tough skin. Their doubt just made me push myself even more.

We used the house of Carlito, a studio owner, in Murietta Hot Springs, to do the photo shoot for the "Stranded" album cover. A red Lamborghini sat in the driveway, the house was huge, and the grounds stretched over a couple of acres. There were living quarters for the help which were probably bigger than what most two-income households owned. He had horses on the land. The grounds looked like a huge, beautiful park. I was in awe. We went to a room in the front of the house for the photo shoot – to give us that whole rap persona of living a big life. I sat on the sofa overlooking the grounds and the horses. Everything went well that day and the cover was great.

Most of the project was recorded at Tony G's studio. Tony G and Julio G were big in the radio industry at the time. We met Tony G through Buzz. Tony had engineered for a lot of the major rap groups back in the day, and while he was engineering the project, he told us stories about when he produced for NWA before they split up.

As we sat in the studio, out of the blue Tony said, "Triece, I have a reading for you." My face wrinkled up baffled that this cool rap producer would be talking about a reading. Before I could answer, Tony said, "It's a gift I was born with. Do you want to hear it?"

"Sure." I said.

"In spite of your hard work, there's a lot of negativity around this project. Some people don't want it to happen. I had a vision last night that Rodney is going to sabotage this project. He needs to be the center of attention. You are gaining respect out there in the industry; everyone feels you are leading the operation. Rodney will never be able to accept that. He is going to turn on you and cause you a lot of pain. You won't be able to recover from it. You should give him these masters and walk away while you can. The longer you stay, the worse your fall will be. You'll see." I sat in the studio listening and waiting for him to finish. My exterior demonstrated my calm composure, but inside his words troubled me. But, I shook it off. "I'll do whatever you need for the sake of Buzz. He's like family, and this project has given him confidence. He used to be really quiet but now he is assertive and very excited about this opportunity. That's the only reason why I'm going to finish up."

I was surprised, but not shocked, that he had just spewed all of that out to me. I didn't know which scared me more. "Thank you for that reading and thank you for seeing the project through; but Glen would never do anything like that to me. We're closer than most cousins, more like brother and sister." I didn't know what else to say after that. I was going full steam ahead. What people didn't know was that once I made my mind up about something, it would be hard to deter me from accomplishing what I set out to do. Besides, Glen and I were "thick as thieves"; he would never do anything to hurt me.

Later that same day, I called my assistant, Francis, to tell her what Tony G said. She said, "Well, I have some friends that do readings too. Do you wanna go?" I told her "No." Everyone thought all the money was coming from the so-called big settlement Glen had received, which the majority was; but a lot of his money was tied up in legal crap too – legal battles with the lawyers or ex-wives or some other nonsense. I was not just riding Glen's coattails; I was in this up to my freakin' neck. I may not have had the money Glen had, but what little I had, I had invested in this project. I had a lot to lose and I hadn't planned on losing. I had been through too much and Glen had been through more than any human should have ever had to endure. It was time for something positive to emerge out of all that hardship. It was time for us to show the world we both were still standing, regardless of how it had tried to break us down.

I began having a series of meetings with record executives, all of whom thought the project was good. My assistant, Francis, or Carolyn would attend these meetings with me. The music industry was cutthroat, so we traveled in pairs for safety.

Francis and I drove out to the valley to meet with a producer to hear some music, but he flaked out on us, so we had time to kill. Francis said, "Triece, we're not far from the readers I told you about. Let's go check them out."

"Girl, I don't even believe in that crap," I said. But we had nothing to do so we went. There were two different readers within a block of each other. We went into the little blue house of the first one. The house, from the outside, looked like a blue dollhouse with white trimmings. I was embarrassed to even walk in the door. Inside, there was a desk with some jars of something weird in it and the smell of incense burning. I thought, *What the hell am I doing in here?* A lady with an accent popped from behind the wall in back of the desk. "Hello Francis, and who might you be?" I thought, *you're the one with the reading skills, you tell me who I am?*

Before I could tell her my name, Francis blurted, "This is my friend, Ontresicia."

"Oh, what a beautiful name," she said in her now obviously fake accent.

"She would like a reading today," Francis blurted out again.

"Come right in," the little lady said as she took my hand and guided me to a small room through an open door just behind the front room we had entered. She sat down behind the desk and started flipping cards over, studying each of them. All I could think was, *I hope she can't read my mind.* When she finished, she looked at me and said, "A family member you are very close to will cause you a great deal of pain and suffering. You need to cut your ties and remove yourself from this person immediately. You love this person dearly, but the longer you stay, the more pain you will have." She freaked me out. I pulled a ten-dollar bill out of my wallet, said "thank you" with a half smile, got up, and walked out.

Francis ran after me. "Ontresicia, don't be upset."

I turned around to her as we reached the car and said, "I'm not upset, I don't even believe in that stuff, but did you tell her about Tony G's prediction?"

"No. I didn't. This was a bad idea, so let's go. Forget the other one."

"No. Let's hear it," I said.

We went to the other reader and she went through the same process, but her outcome was different. She told me that this family member loved me and needed me desperately to help protect him. If you do not stay with him, he will endure great pain. I paid her and left. Although I didn't believe in the readings, they troubled me.

A few days later, Carolyn and I were scheduled to meet with Rod Linnum – a VP at Universal. We went into the huge glass building and selected the sixth floor after entering the elevator. We walked up to the receptionist.

"Hi, I'm Ontresicia, here to see Rod Linnum." She checked her schedule.

"You can have a seat. I'll let him know you're here."

"Thank you." Carolyn and I sat down.

The reception area was very elegant. The receptionist sat behind a huge cherry wood counter in a plush soft leather chair. At the far end of the room was a high-end coffee and cappuccino maker that sat on a huge desk matching the receptionist's counter. Even the trash can looked expensive. As I sat there admiring the luxury of it all, Carolyn nudged me. My name had been called.

"Oh, OK." I rushed up to follow the receptionist into Rod's office. His office made the reception area look average in comparison. As I entered, the first thing I noticed was the view from the wall-to-wall window behind his massive shiny black lacquered desk.

"Hi." He had to walk around the desk to shake my hand.

"I'm happy to finally meet you in person. This is my business associate Carolyn," I said while pointing to Carolyn. We both sat down on the opposite side of his desk. To the left his walls were draped with awards, accolades, and framed gold and platinum records. To the right was a matching hutch with carved leather insets on both pieces of furniture. The crown molding gave the already grand furniture a royal touch.

Rod said, "Great project!" while bobbing his head. We had been waiting to hear it. No one expected it to be this good. I'll hand it to my promoters so they can give me some feedback from the street."

Yay! Carolyn and I were bubbling with the excitement of possibly nailing a production deal. We were doing it. I was taking care of the business and Glen handled the creative side of this partnership. What could go wrong? I could remove those readings from my mind. We chatted about the business a tad longer and left the building on a natural high.

My next meeting was with an executive from SEMA. My heart skipped a beat when he said, "Excellent project," but it was evident from the tone that there was an unspoken "but" that followed. The next words that came out of his mouth struck like a double-edged sword.

"Now, you need to consider removing Rodney's name from it. The two people everyone hates the most are Rodney King and O.J. Simpson." He continued. "Great project, wrong name. And packaging – repackage the product. We can sell it."

My friend Carolyn had accompanied me to this meeting. After she listened to what the executive said, she was furious.

"How can he say that? He doesn't even know Rodney. I just don't understand why these people keep criticizing him, like he is some kind of monster," she yelled.

This was not the first time I heard this, but I had also heard so many compliments like "Great project….Excellent…. Sound goods", that I didn't focus on the other distribution companies that wanted me to remove Glen's name from the project. I hadn't told Glen of any of this because I knew first-hand what would happen if he started stressing. He was in a good place and I wanted him to stay there. The world needed to see this side of Glen. And where did they get off comparing him to O.J.? He hadn't been accused of murdering anyone. He was the victim of a horrendous crime that everyone witnessed. This time it affected me. The comment slapped me in the face, and I became livid with these people for putting him down after he had worked so hard to pull this together, to this level, having never been in the industry. Trust me, he didn't get there because of his name alone. As a matter of fact, his name probably did more harm than good. But still, I thought, *whatever, we're still moving forward.*

As time went on, money was going out, but it was never enough. The music industry proved to be a much tougher vault to crack into.

Everybody wanted money, money, and more money in order for you to get radio time. I met with several radio producers to pitch the Stranded Project. Most of them had no problem getting the music in a rotation as long as the money was right. I was told over and over again how various rappers who had big contracts had paid out thousands of dollars or how they had bought this one and that one a boat or some other toy of equal or higher value.

A president of a large music store wanted us to take on another artist who had been big at one time but now was struggling. If we did, she said she would personally push our project buying large amounts of CDs. Well, I told her that we didn't have the money to take on another artist now. We were putting everything into Stranded but she didn't seem to care. She said she would buy some of our product, but she would be pushing another group that was coming out at the same time if we didn't take on her artist. She put it out there to me just like that.

One evening, Glen and John met her and our publicist for a dinner meeting. I wondered why Glen would be meeting with her, because for months now I had handled all of the negotiating and meetings.

About a week later, I was at John and Carolyn's house, and John told me the woman told Glen that he needed to go national, for that was the only way he would really make any money. She also told him that his cousin (me) didn't know what she was doing. John said the woman said all sorts of negative things about me to Glen and he never once defended me. I thought, *Glen didn't even know this woman and he allowed her to talk about me like that.*

After that meeting, Glen was bent on going national. This was a whole new ball game. We had to start hiring a slew of promoters in other states to get to the national level. We had already hit a brick wall in California with the single. They wouldn't put it into the radio rotation. It was almost like starting from scratch. Also, I had to pay huge amounts of money to promoters, from our marketing budget, so they would get the word to the program directors to set-up radio promotion nationally.

We hadn't really gotten the project off the ground the way Glen expected and he was getting depressed and impatient. His enthusiasm was starting to wither, but I refused to let it go. After all he had gone through? I refused to let him lose again. I was on a mission to help him recoup the money he had lost to all of the greedy lawyers. Also, we had worked too hard on this project to just give up. Like I said, I also had a personal interest as well – to get something for my investment.

Straight Alta-Pazz Records finally inked a distribution deal with Paulstarr Distributing, a company that worked with many independent labels. We signed a one-year deal, after which either party would be able to renegotiate. We were excited about getting this deal because Paulstarr had a reputation of only dealing with very promising projects, regardless of who was behind them. Despite Tony G's warning, everything was looking good.

One of our biggest achievements was managing to get news coverage of Glen and the group rapping during prime time news. This was considered "Big Willie" style. No rappers had ever had that type of coverage on prime time news. That piece of the promotion earned me a serious stripe from some of the veteran rappers. Snoop was impressed. His manager, Steve Saber, contacted me and Snoop Dogg sent some of his friends over to my office to help with the project. I was told by some street promoters that I was the only lady at an independent record label running a project. Even Eazy's wife, Tamika, wasn't allowed to run the company and projects, according to the promoters we used.

We were losing steam, but I found out about a promoter named Bill Johnson through a mutual friend. He was expensive but highly recommended, so I spoke to our distribution company to coordinate getting the music in the stores ready for purchase while he was promoting on radio. He said he needed the money up front to set up his travel arrangements and other arrangements. I said, "OK, but wait to hear from me before you go down there because I have to make sure the music will be in the stores ready to purchase." A couple of weeks went by and he called me saying he had returned from down south where he had run his promotion campaign for the Stranded Project. I couldn't believe what I was hearing. This man had gone to all the southern states from Alabama to Louisiana before he heard from me. He had a full blown-out promotion campaign for the group, had gotten radio time, had the people there requesting the music on the radio, and they had no music in the record stores. That was the most painful forty thousand dollar lesson I had ever learned. I, too, began to feel this project was not going to make it. Almost the entire budget Glen had set aside for the promoting and marketing for this project was gone.

Luckily for us, I had created quite a buzz. One day when I was feeling quite defeated by the last ordeal, a man named Wesley Jackson from Sumter, South Carolina called me to ask if I would be willing to manage a group for him. I told him I really didn't have the funds to take on another group at the time and that I was trying to promote our project at the radio stations. I told him about Stranded. He then told me he had heard about them. That lit up my world. He said in the sweetest southern twang, "Well, my family owns almost all of the radio stations down here, from North Carolina down to right before Atlanta." I was leisurely lying on the sofa but I jumped up and dashed over to the desk to grab pen and paper and prepare to take down as much information as I could from this angel who had been sent to me. He continued, saying, "Maybe we can work out something else."

Come to find out, he was a city worker, but he messed with music on the side – his real passion. He was very interested in meeting Rodney King. He just wanted Glen to be there for interviews and be at their annual parade that was coming up in a few months. Wesley really wanted Rodney to be in this parade. He was so excited, he said he would have the media folks take pictures, conduct interviews, and then talk to the concert folks so that Stranded could perform. He said, "If Rodney and the group come for that, I will get you on all of the radio stations from North Carolina to Orangeburg, South Carolina – which was a college town, stopping at Georgia." It felt as if new life had been breathed into the project. If we could tap into that area, everything else would indeed fall into place.

Around this time, Glen had begun acting strange. He was not himself. He had become cold and distant and had started questioning me about the money I was spending on the project. I thought this would get us back to where we were, as a family. I explained to him, in detail, what Wesley Jackson expected of us in order for this deal to happen. It seemed to perk him up a little. The group was excited, and I was on a cloud somewhere because I fully understood the magnitude of this opportunity.

A few months later, I was purchasing the airline tickets for Glen and the group. We had been making plans since the day of the call from Wesley. It was time for them to perform in South Carolina for the town's big event, and Wesley had made a name for himself for getting this group – Rodney King's group – to their local shindig. He had confirmations from newspaper reporters and local news stations with cameramen. This was huge. Meanwhile, Glen had been traveling back and forth to Sacramento and was still being difficult – hanging out with all sorts of women that lacked integrity and morals. He was just not professional...still not himself. As angry as I was with him, I knew part of his actions were due to the pressure everyone had put on him, and even the stress he had put on himself when he formed this record label. So, I was still determined to make this happen. He would be strong again, because he had taught himself and learned so much. It couldn't all be in vain. And yes, I still wanted to show those lawyers and everyone who turned on him that they wouldn't break him. Rodney Glen King would prevail.

The group left on Thursday night, and Glen was supposed to meet up with them later on. Before Glen left for the airport, I told him how important it was that he not be late to the airport. He couldn't afford to miss his plane, so I told him to go directly to the airport. I was a surrogate mom all over again.

The next day, Buzz called me and told me Wesley was very upset.

"Why?" I asked.

"Rodney didn't show up. He's not here and Wesley is really mad."

I wanted to just crawl up under a rock somewhere and disappear.

Minutes after I hung up the phone, Wesley called. Again in the sweetest southern twang he said, "Ontresicia, Rodney is not here. I have all these people here to see him and he's not here." By the time everyone knew Glen wasn't there, it was too late to reschedule anything or make calls to anyone. "Now, I told you I would get your music in rotation on all of the radio stations, but I won't be doing that now. We will still have the concert Saturday night but that's it."

Glen eventually showed up. He was there later that night and attended the concert but by then, Wesley had faced total humiliation and embarrassment.

When Glen returned home, he said, "The people down there were so nice, everything was…"

I immediately cut him off and said, "Glen, I know you didn't make it there on time. Wesley called me, so you can stop acting like everything went okay." I was beyond livid with him. I berated him for what seemed like hours as he moped around rubbing his brow and looking confused about his own actions. My life had changed completely. I had graduated from college and was no longer at JPL. My security blankets were gone. I had been working full-time to get this project off the ground. We had spent the first year researching and learning the music business; now, it seemed it was coming to an end.

The official release date for the Stranded album was April 29, 1998. Exactly six years after the L.A. riots. This seemed to mean more to me than anyone else. This was our memorial for that horrible day. It was supposed to be a day of recognition and atonement, but we were so busy trying to promote this project, the day went by barely noticed for its history.

I spent the remainder of my personal money I had allocated for the project to promote the album in South Carolina and Atlanta. However, my money wasn't quite enough to send the group there again to perform and do radio which was crazy because finally the music was in the stores. I couldn't rely on the street promoters doing a good job posting the posters in the stores or getting spins in the clubs because I couldn't see them. I no longer believed their status updates on the Monday morning conference calls or the lousy pictures they'd send at the end of the week illustrating where they had posted the promotion items. The music started selling in South Carolina, which was odd because the Southeast was more geared towards East Coast rap. But everybody in the south and east coast just loved Glen to death. They had been waiting for the music to arrive at the stores ever since Glen and the group made the trip out there. It was all due to my key contact, Wesley Jackson. He was a good guy. Real honest. Within a couple of weeks the stores were sold out of the product. However, it had passed the 90 day period of the initial distribution date, so the product was considered dead from a distributor's point of view. I took a chance and called Paulstarr and asked them to fill the stores again in South Carolina. According to them, they had already distributed the entire product that the major record stores preordered. At this point, if more product was needed, the stores would have to go to the One Stops, the large music warehouses, to buy the product. The nearest One Stop in the south that Paulstarr shipped to was in Georgia, so the retailers were on their own if they really wanted the music. Anyway, I decided to worry about that later. I was elated to hear all the music had sold, so I rushed to notify Glen.

"Glen! Glen!" I shouted. I ran down the long hallway and made a sharp left turn to his bedroom door. I banged on his door. "Glen! Open up!"

He cracked his door, "What you want, Cous?"

"Guess what?" Before he could answer I continued. "The music has sold out in Sumpter, SC and the music is getting high radio rotation on its own merit." Wesley said he would still get the music on his local station but the deal to get the music played in the other areas was off because of Glen's no show for the media he had planned. "I just got the report from the station. It's catching!" I said. Actually the music sold well in Pasadena, Covina, West Covina, Wherehouse records, and surrounding mom-and-pop stores in Los Angeles without radio play. The sales momentum had begun, but I was out of product in the areas that needed it.

He opened the crack in his door a little more, there was a slight grin on his face, but it suddenly changed to a snarl. "I want all of my mothafuckin' money first. In fact, I want all the money, and I'll decided how much you'll get. You understand that Cous? I want all of my shit first!" He yelled.

I knew Glen hadn't been himself in a long time, even before the launch of the project, he began changing. It was because of all of the other cases he had lost, and the money he spent to fight them was astronomical. He had to spend some time in county jail for a month or so for some charge he was convicted on. He was drinking more and more, his personality and mood changed, almost, every 60 seconds or so whenever you were in his company. Needless to say, I was pissed at him too. I thought about how this was his dream, and he became too self-destructive to help me with his personal business and the record label. I had asked him to do one thing – to make himself available when it was time to promote the album. He failed to do that, and then had the nerve to tell me that he wanted his money first. In fact, all of it! I was steaming, "What about my money, Glen?" I replied. "What about the years I've spent developing this company, cleaning-up your name in the media, handling your affairs, keeping you out of trouble, doing all the major work for this project while you lay up in the bed all damn day screwing all of these no-good women? What do you mean you want all of your money first? Straight Alta-Pazz Records belongs to both of us. You didn't finance this alone, and you sure as hell haven't done your share of the work. So what the fuck do you mean?" By the time I had regurgitated all I had done with little to no help from him, I had lost control.

He looked at me, swung his door open all the way, and said, "You know what, fuck that little money of yours, it's nothin in comparison to my money. Nothing. You hear me, Cous? Nothin!" At that time, I could understand why he decided not to invest anymore money in the project. It was the grand idea of the publicist who brainwashed him and told him that the project needed to go national in the first place. I told him we could not afford to sign a group, make an album, and market and promote nationally on $100- $150K, which was our budget. I knew that we didn't have the manpower or financial resources to do it. But still, he insisted, and threatened to hire the publicist to take over the record label. My thought was, she may take over your part, but she won't be taking a damned thing from me.

The constant bickering became the norm throughout the rest of the time we worked the project. Everyone wanted to be a part of his life. Some wanted the money, and others just wanted to say they knew him. The elation from that report soon diminished after my argument with Glen. A couple of the stores traveled to the One Stops to get more music, but not enough. I felt drained, but not enough to give up – even if I couldn't work with Glen.

I received another call. This time, it was from Carolyn. She told me she had heard of this big street promoter in Atlanta named Casper. Stanley, John's friend, was the radio promoter. She heard from a reliable source that he had strong connections and could definitely get us radio time. I had a little money left in my retirement account, so against my better judgment, I contacted Casper and we worked out a deal. This time, I made sure the album was in all the music stores first, then I paid him to promote the Stranded Project. Needless to say, it was a bust.

Chapter Twelve
A Family in Turmoil

A fter the last attempt in Atlanta, I felt the Stranded Project was truly over, although neither of us had officially said it. Glen had gone to northern California a couple of times to visit the rest of our family. Each time he returned, the anger had escalated to a new level. One day, out of the blue, he asked me, "Do you have any of my personal checks?" and then asked, "When's the last time you've talked to Tim Voytko?", his financial manager.

I said, "Why are you asking me crazy questions like that? Have I ever had your personal check book? And why in the hell would I be calling Tim Voytko?" I told him, "I don't know what you are trying to ask me, but I don't like it." I was so pissed off that I told Carolyn about it, and she told her husband John. It turns out, Carolyn told me that John had been around Glen on occasions and heard him telling people that his cousin, Triece, manages all of his affairs as well as his money. John said this is what Glen would tell people and family members that he didn't want to lend money to. Now, I did manage his business affairs, but not his personal money – only the money that he gave me to put into the household and business accounts. Even when managing his business affairs, we never had a signed agreement for me to be his business manager. He just needed help, and I was the family member that he asked to help. As far as the business of the Stranded Project, that was me managing our project and the record label.

Not long after the beating, Aunt Dessa and Tasha moved back to northern California. She felt southern California brought too many problems – too many bad things happened here. So, Glen visited them often, and it seemed he needed deprogramming every time he returned.

One day, we were at home. I was in the office and he walked in and said, "We can't go on with the project, I don't have no more money to put into it."

I was reading some articles. I put the paper down and said, "Well, I understand Glen. If it was up to me I would've stopped after the first thirty thousand we lost – when I told you initially that we shouldn't move forward. But we did, and then you decided to go national, which I couldn't understand. But I'm going to try to breathe some life into a small regional area. I have some more money left, so I'll pump it in a smaller region to see if I can recoup something."

At this point, we had burned through a lot of money and were planning on moving to a smaller house in Fontana. Although things were really bad between us, I couldn't move out because I had no where else to go.

One day I was talking to Glen's other aunt, Gail, and she told me that my aunt Dessa said, "I was spending all of Glen's money."

So I knew then that this was much worse than I thought. Then, my own sister called me one day and said, "Hey Triece. So I heard you just stole Glen's money," while giggling as if this was some sort of joke.

"What? Stole Glen's money?" I said.

"That's what everybody is saying out here," speaking of Sacramento. I was so hurt. Tears filled my eyes. I plopped down on my bed. I felt the blood drain from my face. I thought I would pass out. I just hung the phone up. I knew my sister didn't believe that, but I don't think she knew how deeply painful it was to hear that my own family would think I was even capable of doing such a thing.

When Glen came home that night, I questioned him about it. By this time, I was overheated and hurt, so I'm not sure how I must have approached him. I met him at the door, and as soon as the door opened, I said, "Glen, are you going around telling people I stole your money?"

"What are you talking about, Cous?"

"I want to know because that's what I'm hearing from the family." I yelled.

"Cous, I would never say anything like that about you. I ain't said nothing like that," he said.

At that point, as far as I knew he still had plenty of money, so why would he be spreading these vicious rumors? A couple of years prior, we were at the tennis court, and after our game we were talking about the reason he didn't want to invest money in construction, which is the business he had worked in. It was because our uncle, Wesley, and my cousin, Paul, (Glen's baby brother), did not get along very well. They were the two who were general contractors, but he didn't trust that they could work together. The two of them made it clear that they didn't want to work with each other. So, Glen chose the music industry, but he was a little scared. He made the joke, "You know if it don't work, I'ma blame it all on you." Of course I didn't take him seriously, I just laughed, "yeah right." But suddenly, I remembered conversations like that, and what Tony G had predicted. It seemed liked Glen had done everything possible to sabotage the project.

Then I remembered a year ago while at my cousin John's wedding, another cousin, Morgan, and I were talking about the music industry. He was drinking a coke and he looked at me and said, "So why in the hell would you convince Glen to invest in music?"

I said, "I didn't, it was his idea. I believed in it, so I invested in it." He said, "Right." Looking at me as to say, 'I'm supposed to believe that?' Then he said, "That's some stupid shit you did." He threw the rest of his coke onto the ground and shook his head while walking away.

I started getting flashes of all sorts of conversations with family members, passersby, and friends. I had been too busy to absorb the negativity around me, but it was all staring me in the face now.

He never admitted to anything. I could see the "writing on the wall" that I needed to get the hell out of there, but I had nowhere to go. I was trapped. I didn't like that feeling at all. It reminded me too much of JPL.

Around June of 1998, the family in northern California was throwing a huge family reunion. We hadn't had one since we were kids, when Grandma Roses was alive. There had been so many ugly things said between Glen and me that I decided I wouldn't go. I could not ride up north with him in the same truck. Why would I go there anyway? I knew people were talking about me.

When Glen returned, he told me that my biological dad and his brother made an appearance at my mom's family reunion. I had seen him maybe four times in my entire life. He never wanted anything to do with me before, but he thought he'd surprise me. That seemed very suspect to me. Glen was very excited...much more than I. He described to me what he looked like.

"Oh Cous, you should have came."

I told him why I didn't go. I explained that I was tired of arguing with him and hearing the lies being told. Again, he swore he had nothing to do with any of it. Things simmered down a bit, for a while, but he continued his self-destructive path of drinking and whatever else.

One day we were able to have a calm conversation and I told him, "Glen, you've got to get a handle of yourself. You can't destroy yourself."

He replied, "I'm not you, Cous. I've tried it your way. My little friends aren't perfect like you either. They can't clean up like you or do all the other things you do. You make people feel bad with all of your expectations. This is my life...my money...and I've got one life to live. This is how I'm going to live it. Do you understand that?"

"OK, I do understand. I'm going to need some time to find a job, either in entertainment or back in corporate America. As soon as I get a stable job, I will leave."

"You don't have to leave."

"No. I will. I think that'll be best."

Meanwhile, one day while I was out running errands, I saw a business acquaintance Glen and I had met several years back. I'll call him Tyler. I was excited to see him, and it turned out that the feeling was mutual.

He said, "Oh my goodness, I've heard so much on the radio and news about the Stranded Project. You and Glen must have made lots of money. I knew this would work. I'm proud of you guys."

Glen was the last person I wanted to talk about right then. I said, "Well, it could have worked, but there are some issues we need to iron out. In fact, with your legal background, maybe you can help me."

He said, "Well, I'm on sabbatical. I'm not practicing these days, but why don't you stop by my place so we can talk about it over tea." He wrote down the address and handed it to me. Wow! We had a connection that I had never noticed in the prior years. That Saturday, I stopped by his Brentwood penthouse. It was beautiful. He was a clean-cut, well dressed, chocolate man with a chiseled jaw line, a clef in his chin, and big brown eyes. He smelled good too. As I was drinking my tea, sitting on his sofa, dressed in Calvin Klein Jeans and Dan Post Cow Boy Boots, I thought, *it's been a long time since I've even noticed a man. Boy does he smell good.* Out of nowhere I blurted, "Excuse me, but what's the name of the cologne you're wearing?"

He replied, "Oh, its Jean Paul Guittier."

"Oh, I like that," I said calmly, but I wanted to jump him right then. I thought, *let me end this meeting quickly so I'll have a reason to come back.* So I did.

"Okay, I don't mean to rush, but I have another appointment. I'll fill you in quickly." I talked about the money disagreement between Glen and me, but I didn't go into details. We made arrangements to meet again within a week or so.

It was Saturday, but this time it was early evening. The concierge buzzed me into the garage, and I parked. I hopped out of my car wearing a white, haltered, Marilyn Monroe Moschino dress. It had black, newspaper print writing in French all over the white fabric. On the elevator, I pushed Penthouse. When the door opened, Tyler stood there dressed in a classic Armani suit, and said, "I was hoping we could discuss the rest of your business over dinner. He looked down at my dress and began reading the fine, French print and interpreting it in English for me. Then, he looked up and said, "I've made reservations for six o'clock at a French restaurant in Westwood."

My heart was beating fast, but this time for all of the right reasons. "That's fine with me. It's a beautiful evening." We hopped in his Benz and were on our way to Westwood.

When we arrived at the restaurant, the valet opened the door for me. When I stepped out, the wind blew the bottom of my dress up, just a bit. Tyler walked around to my side of the door, gazed into my eyes, and said, "You look amazingly, beautiful."

He held my hand and we walked into the restaurant. I thought, *ok, what are you really doing?* This was feeling like a real date, not a business meeting. Here I thought I'd get to his place and coerce him into dinner; but no, he had already planned dinner. Hmmm. I thought, *Glen is going to kill me.* This was someone he knew and admired. *I just won't tell him. He doesn't need to know my business anyway.* We were no longer using this man's professional service, so why should he care. Besides, it had been years since I'd been in the presence of a man on a personal level. As we were looking at our menus, I felt people staring at us. I knew I was wearing that Moschino dress. My body was to die for: well-toned, tight, and curvy – all in the right places for that dress. But they weren't looking at me. At least not all of them.

An elderly white gentleman to the right of me came over to our table and introduced himself. He said, "Mr. Tyler, I just want to tell you, how much I admire and respect your work. I've been following your career since you first began practicing law in England. I think you're brilliant and your wife here is just stunning." Then, he kissed my hand. The two continued in quick small talk and the gentleman went back to his table. It was the most relaxing evening I'd had in years.

Finally, I had a life outside of work, school, music, and Glen. As months passed, we became romantically involved. Tyler became my weekend getaway. Sometimes, a weekend would pass and we'd never leave the house. I'd feed him grapes, crackers and cheese; and we'd drink tea, sparkling cider, and of course sometimes I'd have a glass of chardonnay. He didn't drink, smoke, use profanity or intake anything unhealthy to his body. That's what I loved the most about him. He had a sense of purity, but he wasn't judgmental. He also had a great sense of humor. I didn't want him to know about the bickering between Glen and me because he was very fond of us both. I think we reminded him of the relationship he and his sister had.

Months had passed, so I could no longer keep the secret that Glen and I were not getting along. I told him I had been working temp jobs and trying to pay off the debt I used to leverage some of the manufacturing and shipping before we got a distribution deal. I was badly in debt, and Glen had surrounded himself with destructive women and friends. I couldn't save him. Tyler was very supportive and understanding. We were connecting in every way.

The new girl Glen was dating was practically living with us. I didn't really have an appreciation for her because I felt she was no good for him. They would spend hours locked in the room, and I became suspicious of the activity that may have been going on. I began to question Glen a lot – like a mother. I guess, to get me off his back, he started implying that I had spent too much of his money on the project.

"You spent all the mothafuckin' money," he yelled.

I knew this was not Glen's personality so all of this was very painful for me to listen to. Things got worse, because either Glen was taking this kind of information to the family or they were feeding it to him. Something was very wrong. I knew he told people I was handling his money, but this went to a new height.

One day, prior to moving to Fontana, his younger brother, Paul, came over to the house in Upland and said, "So, y'all little project is over, so when you leavin? And when you leave you better not try to take that expensive bed Glen bought that you're sleeping on."

I said, "Hold up one minute. Glen didn't purchase this bedroom set. As a matter of fact, everything in here was purchased with my own money."

"This is my five to six thousand dollar stuff," I said while waving my finger at everything in the room, "and when I go, it goes."

This must have bothered him to know I wasn't about to be punked like that, so he came back with, "I want to see an account of all that money you spent."

I couldn't believe that this nonsense was coming from my little cousin who I loved. This was when I truly realized my family was definitely talking about me – accusing me of basically being a thief. Could Glen have actually been spreading these rumors about me? And how much had really been said? What were people saying? If my own family could think such horrible things, what were others outside of the family thinking and saying? Somehow, I felt that Glen's mind was being poisoned against me because this was not my cousin. He wouldn't say anything like that. But, if the family was saying these things about me, why didn't he defend me?

The week we were packing to move to Fontana, Glen and I got into a huge argument. One of our cousins said that when Glen was in Sacramento, some of the family was talking to him about how I just went through all of his money. I asked Glen why he was allowing people to talk about me like that. He yelled, "I'm sick of this shit, I can't control what people say."

"You can't control them but you sure as hell can stick up for me and defend me when you hear shit that's not true." I was tired; we had been packing all week. I believed Glen didn't want me to move to Fontana with him, but he didn't have the heart to tell me.

In Fontana, the rumors about me spending all of Glen's money had gotten worse. His children's mothers began claiming that I just took his money and bought the kids extravagant clothes and things that they didn't need. I was "just using Rodney's money", they'd say. No one was ever happy with me. I was either doing too much or not doing enough. They claimed Glen had bought all of my clothes. This had passed being ridiculous.

One of Glen's ex-girlfriends I still spoke to on occasion told me Glen's aunt, Ann was spreading rumors that I was sleeping with Glen. The first time I had heard a rumor like that was a couple of years prior. At that time, his girlfriend was upset because she wasn't invited to go on the business trips with us; so she started rumors that I must have been sleeping with Glen. I didn't think twice about it because the women he chose to have relationships with were not people I needed to think twice about. Besides, people knew me and they knew my character – or I thought. But now, this was family.

Although Ann wasn't my blood, I still respected her as my aunt too. Could money make people lose their minds like this?

One day in March of 1999, I had plans to drive to LA that evening to see Tyler. Glen's daughter, Candace who was about fifteen at the time, was there for a few days and, like I said, Glen's girlfriend, I'll call Regina, practically lived with us. Early evening, I told Candace I was going to take a nap but for her to wake me at 8:00 p.m.

"Ok Triece. I'll wake you up." It was a draft in the house, so I went to my room, jumped into bed and pulled the comforter over my shoulders and fell asleep.

I was awakened by shouting, "Candace! Candace! Open the door!"

There were three rapid bangs on his bedroom door and I could hear a sense of urgency or fear in Glen's voice. Suddenly, I heard a big, BAM! The door flew open and from the sound of it, hit the wall.

"Open the damned door! What the hell are you doing in my bedroom with my daughter and the door is locked? You don't lock no fuckin' doors up in this house! You understand that?" Glen yelled at his girlfriend.

"What? Why are you screaming at us?" Candace shouted back.

"What? We was just layin' here talkin' on the phone, that's all." Regina responded.

"Well if you were just layin' here, why didn't you open the damned door, huh? I told Candace to go to sleep hours ago." Glen said.

"She was sleep. She had just fallen asleep not long ago," Regina replied.

"Oh, first y'all was just layin' here talkin' on the phone, and now the story is Candace was sleep," he mocked her. "You tellin' a damn lie. I tell you what, you get your shit and get up out of my house. You came with your brother- in-law and you leavin' with him." I was still in my room listening. Then I heard, bang! It sounded like the closet door hitting the wall. I heard rattles like he was snatching clothes from out of the closet.

"Here take all of this funky ass shit and get out!" Glen yelled.

"I'm not goin' nowhere, plus you can't tell me what to do Rodney," Regina boasted.

"What? Are you out of your fuckin' mind? Did you hear what I said?" I guessed she was feeling very confident that her brother-in-law, I'll call Wayne, would come into the room and diffuse the situation or defend her, but I never heard his voice.

Glen walked down the hallway into the living room. I heard him say, "Man, you gotta leave and take her with you, I mean it." On that note, I came out of my bedroom and went into the living room. I saw a pint of Cognac sitting on the living room table. Our cousin, Damien, was sitting on the sofa Wayne was sitting on the living room chair across from Damien. The men were quiet, Glen was standing up, and Candace and Regina were still in the room grumbling about whatever had just happened.

I looked at Damien and said, "Cousin, what just happened and what time is it?"

"Uh, it's a little after 1:00 a.m." Damien said.

"Cous, she was in my bedroom with my baby and the door was locked. I banged and banged on the door and they wouldn't open it." Glen said still fuming.

"I don't understand why you are so mad." I must have looked as confused as I was because Glen began explaining in detail.

"Well, I went to the store with him," pointing at the brother-in-law, "and Damien. When we came back, we were talking and drinking. A lot of time went by and I realized my girl wasn't in here, and I got a weird feeling that came over me – like something was wrong with Candace. So I went back to my room to make sure she was ok, and the door was locked. Did you hear me knocking on the door?" he asked me.

"Yeah, I did. It woke me up. Candace was supposed to wake me up at 8:00 p.m., but she must have forgotten, and I overslept. Ok, so is everything alright now, Glen?"

"No. It's not alright I was just tellin' them that both of them have to leave, and she can't live here no more."

"Oh, I see." So I walked to his room and asked Candace what happened. Regina was picking up her clothes from the floor and stacking them on the bed.

"He busted in here screaming at us. I'm calling my uncle in Rialto to come and get me." Candace said.

I went back into the living room. "Glen, she has been around your kids for a long time now. What makes this time so different?" I was furious at this point because I had warned him in the beginning about this girl.

"Cous, I didn't want to tell you because I know you'd be mad." Glen said while pacing back and forth shaking his head. Then, he continued, "When you leave to go to work in the morning, a few times, I've caught her in your bedroom and in our office. And you know we keep the office door locked, so I don't even know how she's been getting in there. But I saw her going through our files and paperwork. You know documents with our social security numbers on them along with law suit documents, and other business papers. I don't know what she's been doing in there, but it made me not trust her. And I don't know what she was doing in that bedroom with my daughter either, but she's gotta go, she can't live here no more. It's one thing to sneak around in our business but I'm not letting nobody mess with my girls."

"Ok Glen," I said. I didn't want to make matters worse. I knew her brother-in-law had quite a violent reputation on the streets because she had bragged about some of the violent acts they committed together some years prior. Wayne went into the bedroom to help Regina carry her clothes out of the house, and they left.

Candace came out of the room and told her dad, "I need a ride to Circle K. I called my uncle, and he's gonna pick me up there. I don't want to stay here."

"Damien, take Candace down to the Circle K and wait until her uncle gets there."

"OK Glen," Damien replied. So they left. Damien was gone all of ten minutes when he returned, his eyes were big and he looked nervous and shocked. "Cous, Candace got out of the car and said she would wait for her uncle in front of the store. I waited, watching to make sure she was safe but stayed in the car. Then Regina and Wayne pulls up and tells Candace to get into the car and then they drove off with her," he said excitedly.

"What did you just say, man?" Glen's eyes squinted as he asked while throwing his hands up, "They took my baby? Are you serious? Man, her mom is going to kill me if I don't get Candace back."

"Triece, I've been drinking so I can't drive. Will you drive me to Ontario to get Candace?"

I agreed. "Damien will you ride with us?" I asked.

"Yeah, I'll go with y'all." I went to my room and put on my jeans and boots and drove to Ontario.

When we got to the apartment, Glen went up the stairs, and Damien and I stood behind him. He banged on the door so hard that it rattled the windows next to the door. Then Wayne came to the door. "What do you want man? Why you bang'n on my fuck'in door like that?"

"Nigga, are you crazy? Where's my daughter?" Glen yelled. I had never seen him this furious and I've seen him in many situations. This was a different kind of anger. His child was in danger and nothing else mattered.

The guy said, "Man you can't come up in here." He stood tall and strong, ready to defend his home.

"Nigga move out the way." Glen said while moving from side to side to see if he could see Candace, I guess. Suddenly I stood trembling in fear when I saw the guy pull out a gun pointing it at Glen. I was in shock! So was Damien. Glen started bouncing around Ali style, then stretched out his arms accepting the challenge and said in an unwavering confidence, "Nigga I promise, you can't pull that trigga fast enough!"

"I put this on everythang, Nigga," Wayne said while waving his gun. "Nigga, I put this on Blood," as he threw up his gang sign.

"Naw Motha Fucka. This is on yo black ass." As soon as the word ass left his mouth he grabbed the man's wrist holding the weapon and shouted, "Triece, get Candace out of there."

I frantically ran pass the two men into the apartment shouting, "Candace come out of here right now! Hurry up!" I found her and

Regina hiding in a closet. I grabbed Candace and we ran out of the door and down the stairs. Meanwhile, Glen had managed to out-strength the guy, and the gun had fallen. The guy was about 5′11″ and muscularly built. He was trying to hold his own, but without his weapon, I could see fear on his face as I looked up from the bottom of the stairs. My cousin, Damien, was trying to break-up the fight. I screamed, "Damien, stop them. Oh My God, stop them." Adrenaline was running fast for everyone, especially for Glen. I could see his face, he was enraged. All of a sudden, Glen picked the guy up, like a rag doll, as though he was going to toss him over the banister. I started screaming from the top of my lungs, "Glen stop! Please Stop! You're going to kill him!" I believe the only thing that saved this guy was that Damien panicked and grabbed Glen around his neck, pulling him back and causing Glen to get off balance as he was holding the man. That way, he couldn't toss the guy off the banister. Good thing Damien is 6′4 ½″ – about a half of an inch taller than Glen. His height gave him the leverage needed to pull Glen off balance.

Candace and I ran to the car. A couple of minutes later, Glen and Damien arrived at the car. I was sitting in the driver's seat, crying…and angry that I had driven him to their house. Candace sat in the front passenger seat next to me. Glen and Damien got in the back seat. Glen started yelling at Candace.

"Why did you tell a lie and say your uncle was picking you up Candace?"

I started the car and was about to back-up out of the parking space when all of a sudden, Glen yelled, "Do you hear me talking to you, Candace?" She opened the passenger door and jumped out. She tripped over the curb and fell down.

"Candace, get back into the car." I shouted. She ran away and went back into the arms of the people that her dad was trying to protect her from. I was pretty shaken up. I drove us home and fussed every inch of the way. "Glen you know better. It's your fault that all of this happened. You are the one that keeps exposing the kids to these crazy ass women. I keep telling you to stop it, and you just keep doing it. Why? You're crazy. When I told you that girl was bragging to Dene and Candace about gang bang'n and glamorizing it to them, you never said anything. Now she has stolen Candace's mind. What is that all about? Do you even see the part you've played in this picture?" By the time we got home it was about 4:00 a.m. I went to bed. By sun up, the girlfriend and Candace had gone to the police department and filed charges. I saw pictures of the bruise on her knees from her fall on the curb. I had had enough. By 10:00 a.m., Glen and Damien went to the store to buy orange juice and they met Glen's next girlfriend, all within 6 hours of getting rid of the other one.

It was crazy because somehow Candace and Regina told the police that Glen beat them up because of something I said. I was appalled. A full investigation was launched, and we had to get legal counsel again. To make matters worse, Regina and Candace called Aunt Dessa in Sacramento and told her I was the reason Glen had done all of those things to them. Later, Candace's mom left a message saying, "Glen, if you give me $5,000, we will drop the charges. You wouldn't be in this mess if you hadn't given that bitch, Triece, all of your money." Due to this incident, both she and Glen had to go to family court for custody of Candace. We played this message for the court which assisted in Glen's case against the mom. So, neither of them was awarded custody. Out of everything that had happened, I must say Glen would do anything to protect his girls. He just didn't realize how much of an impact these women would have on them.

A couple of days after the incident, Aunt Dessa called me, yelling and saying horrible things. She accused me of living off of Glen, being jealous of his girlfriends and ex-wives, and all sorts of hurtful things.

I was so fed up, I yelled back. I can't remember everything I said, but I remember telling her, "You don't have a fuckin' daughter-in-law that can even compare to me; just like you could never compare to my mother." I couldn't believe she would tell me I was jealous of any one of those females Glen dealt with. None of them were about anything. Most of them just used him to get what they wanted out of him. I had been trying to protect her son for all of those years and she had the audacity to say some bullshit like that. Even she knew she could always depend on me to help her. I was the first family she called when Glen got in trouble and now this money made her act like this towards me, out of all people. The things this woman, who I considered a second mom, said to me hurt me to the depths of my soul. The room seemed to go dark. I never knew I could feel worse than I felt when I had to face that abuse at JPL, but now it was my own family hurting me like this – spreading vicious rumors about me wanting to be with my own cousin, about being jealous of his women, and about stealing his money! No person should ever have to feel this kind of pain or suffer this kind of betrayal from their family.

After I hung up the phone, I slid down onto the floor in my room and began to sob like a baby. It seemed like I cried for everything I had gone through for the past decade. My entire body endured an indescribable pain. I was trembling uncontrollably. I sat on the floor, bent over with my head buried in my knees. I boo-hooed. My body was just drained. I fell to the floor curled in a fetal position for I don't know how long. I finally turned onto my back and thought, *What had I done so wrong? What was I really guilty of? Because I had to be guilty of something. Did I take on Glen's fight as if it were mine? For that I'm guilty. Was I over-protective of Glen? Guilty. Did I push him so that he could accomplish his dreams? Guilty. Did I believe in him when all others didn't? Guilty. Was I always there for him? Guilty!* I decided right then and there, lying on that floor in my room, that it was time to take care of Triece.

I begin my job search. I found temporary assignments, but the money wasn't good in the Inland Empire. I had to make it back to Pasadena or L.A. to earn a decent wage.

Around this time, I was beginning to experience a lot of pain, and when I went to the doctor I found out I had fibroids. Since I had no medical insurance, I had to go to a clinic. I didn't qualify for welfare because I had too much money, as far as the government's policy was concerned. I had worked all of my life from 14 years old to 36 years old, paying taxes to take care of the poor. Now, I needed help, but the state refused to help me. I was too embarrassed to tell Tyler about my problems. I didn't want him to see me as needy, so I kept it a secret from him for a few more weeks. When I finally told him, by then I needed surgery. He told me not to worry; he would take care of the medical bills.

Instead of going home after my procedure, I went to stay in a hotel. I couldn't face anything or anyone at that time and was in dire need of just a few days of peace and quiet with no tension around me for a change. Although I had shared with Tyler about Glen and me not getting along, I hadn't revealed that my living situation was barely habitable due to the tension. Tyler had a heavy schedule for that week. Since we hadn't planned to be together, I didn't want to ask him to accommodate me for a few days. We were getting close but not live-together close. While in the hotel, I began to look for jobs again. I was desperate, so I looked in all areas. I knew I needed to get out of Glen's house, but I had to get a job first. And even if I got a job, I wasn't sure how fast I could get into an apartment.

I finally had to reach out to long-time friends and some family for help. I tried to get help from my mom, my friend, Leticia, and others; but no one would help me. There was so much gossip flying around about me, but I didn't think my friends who really knew me would believe the rumors. Then again, I never thought my own family would accuse me of what they accused me of either.

The last straw happened when I came back home. As soon as I walked into the door, Glen asked me "Where you been, Cous? Somewhere getting a baby dug out of you?" I just went to my room. For years I had dedicated my life to helping him and now that I was involved with someone who obviously made me happy, all he could think to say to me was something negative like that.

I had started buying clothes for interviews. The ironing board was set up in the family room and I was ironing a skirt I had purchased for an interview that was scheduled for the next day. I saw Glen looking my way, staring at me from my peripheral vision. He said, "Where'd you get that from, Cousin?" He thought I was stripped broke because he knew he had cut me off from the budget. He thought I couldn't even buy groceries. I guess if I didn't have any money to buy myself something to eat, I would have starved since so many people had undoubtedly filled his head with lies about me. I couldn't believe what he was insinuating. I was still sick and hadn't been out of the hospital for more than a week yet.

"What's it to you….you didn't buy it. Doesn't matter where I got something from. All that matters is that you didn't buy it." We argued intensely back and forth. He stood up from the couch where he and his girl were sitting and stood over me, getting very animated. She sat looking with a sinister smirk on her face. I pulled the cord out of the plug and wrapped it around my hand. I was ready for him because I had had enough of the lies and the drama.

I said, "I'll tell you what. If you come any closer to me, when it's all said and done, it's going to be over. You a big nigga and I know you don't care about hitting women back….but I'm your cousin and you talking to me way out of line. Once I get started I won't stop 'til I take you out." I said this as I backed away from the ironing board wrapping the cord around my hand to get in position.

"Cous, you can't swing that mothafuckin' thing quick enough," he said as he started hopping around, entertaining his girl at my expense.

I just looked at him. He was prancing around like he was some big man who was going to take me out. I shook my head, grabbed my skirt, and went into my room. That was the point where I knew I needed to get out, and fast. I couldn't stay where I wasn't sure if I would be safe or not. And the man jumping around in front of me was not someone I recognized. He was a person that I could no longer trust to have my back.

I began looking for a small apartment to rent after that incident. I found a reasonably priced apartment near the Pasadena area and filled out the application. I was devastated when I was turned down due to something on my credit report about another home I had never lived in. It turned out that the townhouse Glen's ex-wife lived in was in Glen's and my name. To hurt him when she left, she destroyed the property. I was beginning to feel like the man Job, from the bible.

After the huge fight with Glen, the project was definitely over, but I had come to enjoy the wheeling and dealing of the industry and felt I had a knack for marketing and promoting. I had become so passionate about the project, I didn't want to let it go.

So, when Mack 10 invited me to the studio to listen to his new group, "Children of the Ghetto," and to observe the different recording techniques and styles, I jumped at the chance. I wasn't sure if anything would come from this meeting. Mack used to tell me that I was too closely involved with the Stranded Project, and that I needed to take time off. He said, "No one person can do everything, Triece. You're just burning yourself out and Glen don't appreciate it."

Before trudging over to the studio that evening, I decided I would cook dinner so Mack and the artist would have a nice, home-cooked meal. Actually, I made a pit stop to Carolyn's house with some chicken wings; marinating in seasoning in a plastic bag. I talked John, Carolyn's husband, into frying the chicken wings for me. Nobody could fry chicken like John.

Carolyn and I arrived at the studio with some homemade yeast rolls, fried chicken, greens, and black eyed peas. The singer singing the hook on one of the projects was the same one who appeared on most of Death Row's projects in the 90's. She said she had been traveling from studio to studio, from the Midwest, non-stop, straight to Cali, singing hooks on rap projects. She was exhausted and hadn't had a home-cooked meal in a month.

I did, however, have other motives. The dinner was really to butter Mack up so that he would put Stranded on his new movie soundtrack, to introduce him to a piece of music from a local artist, and to give him a few other projects handed to me to give to him. At this point, I was reduced to simply peddling music. I was trying hard to stay in the business. It was all I had done since leaving JPL.

That night of my sales pitch to Mack, he told me he wanted to talk to me in private. He's a modest guy, never much of a fuss, just always collecting information before speaking. So we went outside and sat inside of his big, full-bodied, black S600 Benz with butterscotch leather seats. Carolyn climbed into the back seat. He looked over at me and said, "A nigga see you tryin' to stay in the game. Whatchu wanna do, Triece?"

I had told him about the Stranded Project and my fallout with Glen. He had already heard about that on the streets. Regurgitating everything that I had gone through lately, tears began to flow. I was not one to cry easily, but at that time, the tears seemed to flow on a regular – especially when I thought of my family. The gossip and lies that Glen had spread to the family, or the lies he allowed the family to spread, tore through me – slicing my insides like one of those magic slicers you see on late night infomercials. Mack was many years my junior, but so calm and mature for his age; and he always had a wise word to spare.

He continued. "Triece, I'ma tell you somethin'. A nigga didn't think you could pull this shit off, but you surprised me and a lot of other niggas too. Just so you know, I was in New York a few weeks ago promoting Binky's project, All From The I," (this was a group from Inglewood) "and niggas was comin' up to me asking me if I had heard Rodney King's new group, Stranded." He frowned, twisting his face and said, "I said, 'What did you say?'" He told me this had become a common question as he promoted his group, All From The I.

Mack had been very nice to me and allowed Stranded to open gigs for his group, until we could get our feet in the door and stand alone. Anyway, he continued with his pep talk to me saying, "Triece, you took an unknown group from West Covina with no real street credibility and you broke them in market places across the country that are impossible to penetrate. People all over the country, even overseas, have heard of this project." He pointed to his chest and said, "I'm proud of you. I can see that you wanna be in charge of what you're doing, but I think you are good enough to work for a major at this point. I can see you running an entire marketing department. I would like someone like you on my team. And your partner, Carolyn, back there..." he turned around to give her eye contact, "I like your demeanor." Turning back to me he said, "The two of you are a good team together, so don't let Glen or nobody else, as far as that matters, talk shit to you about that project. I want you to hold your head up high, and pop yo collar! And don't be cryin' no more!"

I took his words to heart. I had nothing to be ashamed of and everything to be proud of. I had done what many others could not. But still, this music industry thing was definitely coming to an end for me. If I stayed in this industry, I would want my own company. I'd want full control. Since I couldn't have my own, I turned away, for good this time.

Chapter Thirteen
Back to Corporate America

I knew I had to get back to Pasadena or L.A., so I asked Carolyn and John if I could rent a room from them until I got back on my feet. They said, "Yes." Back in Pasadena, I was able to find work. It was an employer's market, but I found work.

During my stay at Carolyn's house, I was still very angry and hurt about what happened between Glen and me. One day, he popped-up at the house; he said to 'just check on me'. He then broke the news to me that his new girlfriend had been in a car accident while driving his Suburban that was registered in my name, but not for me to worry because he paid the family on the spot. Glen couldn't have an automobile in his name because of his horrible driving record. I agreed to put it in my name and obtain personal insurance for him, so he could drive it. That was years ago. I had really forgotten all about it, until then. I was furious. I was just getting back on my feet. I was working in investment banking at Citibank Private Bank as a temp-to-permanent office manager. Now this. I knew this too, would eventually come back to haunt me.

It was 1999, rap music still had not recovered from the deaths of Biggie and Pac, and no one knew in what direction it was heading. Race relations really had not changed much. At least the economy had improved during the Clinton administration. People seemed to be prospering again. There was a new generation coming up – white, young hip-hoppers who were children in the nineties but grew up hearing and witnessing a great deal of racial strife during the time period. They wanted in, so a lot of known rappers started doing more projects with white artists. Were things finally changing?

Time was moving, before I could blink my eyes, it was the year 2000, and the Republicans were back in office. The Democrats had been in office from the early 90's into the turn of the century. A lot had happened: Magic Johnson had contracted HIV, Michael Jackson was suspected of molesting boys, Michael Jordon had gambling issues and his father had been murdered. President Bill Clinton, often referred to as "our first black President," faced impeachment for lying under oath about his infidelity.

Glen and I hadn't spoken to each other in almost a year until we ran into each other at the hospital visiting Grandpa Mac the night he passed away. I didn't attend the funeral. I loved my grandpa, but I felt my presence at the funeral would have caused an unnecessary disruption in the services – the services that should have focused on him and only him.

In February 2000, I accepted a position in Finance at Philip Morris. A few weeks after I started at Philip Morris, I saw an old friend in the parking lot at Vons Pavilion on Fair Oaks in Pasadena. Ryan Bartlett was his name. It turns out that his cousin, Gina, was married to my cousin, Paul; so Ryan was well aware of my dilemma. Ryan's dad, Ted Bartlett, was a Property Manager and he threw me a lifeline and rented to me, even though my credit was in shambles.

Corporate America had certainly changed since the eighties and nineties. Philip Morris was a very diverse company. I had never seen anything quite like that before. It was nothing like what I was used to at JPL. Maybe enough class action lawsuits had finally brought change to these huge companies.

Philip Morris was impressed with my work history, and not the JPL part of it. They were more impressed that I had run a company in the entertainment industry. I guess something good came out of all that in the end – experience. No one can ever take that away from me. During the interview, they told me that they were looking for leaders - people who had vision and would allow them to develop it. The Western Region VP liked me right away. So did the Senior Finance Director who I would report to.

By April 2000, I was ready to move into my new townhouse in Altadena. Tyler gave me about $5,000.00 for the down payment and other little things I needed. Just when I thought things were looking up, I went to the mailbox, and there was a lawsuit filed against me from the accident Glen's girlfriend had, many months prior. I thought, *this will never end*. I decided to file for bankruptcy and get on with my life. Tyler didn't think that was a good idea, but I didn't care. I had to start living for me.

By July of 2000, Philip Morris put me on the traveling road, back and forth from California to New York, and the in-between states like Texas, Georgia, Jersey, and DC. I was working finance projects, going to leadership conferences, training, and whatever else. Everybody worked themselves to the bone at Philip Morris, but this was a group of people that worked hard and played even harder. It was a very rich company when I started. It reminded me a lot of the lavishness of the entertainment business.

President George Bush, Jr. had won the election, though most believed he didn't really win but stole the election. Rumors flew about a scandal in Bush's Florida campaign office, and people claimed it was one of the biggest acts of electoral fraud – calling it "Floridagate". Bush's leadership would soon be put to the test. Colin Powell was chosen as Secretary of State. Wow! Black people were so proud and happy. We'd never had a black man hold such high office in the White House. For most, it didn't matter what party he belonged to; we just loved the idea that this well-educated, black man was going to be in the position of power – in charge of consulting the President on foreign affairs.

September 10, 2001. I was supposed to have been boarding the 6:50 A.M. United Airlines flight to New York and report to our Park Avenue office on Tuesday, September 11, but I had a premonition that all the traveling was catching up with me. Therefore, I cleared it with the VP to let me sit this trip out. Plus, the pop singer, Aliyah's, tragic death in a plane crash a few weeks earlier had left me a little jittery.

I turned on the television about five-thirty in the morning as I was getting dressed to drive down to the Huntington Beach Hilton to give a presentation to the sales team. As I dried my body and went to dab my underarms with my Bvlgari powder, I was watching Channel 7 News when I saw two planes crash into the Twin Towers. I wasn't sure if it was real time or a replay or what. I immediately turned the TV volume up. I was unsure about what I had just witnessed, until they replayed it again; and this time, I could hear the commentary. I wondered if I had experienced the type of premonition that Tony G had back in the nineties when he gave me that reading.

After the 911 terrorist attacks, we came together as a nation. White, black, brown – it didn't matter – it was all about being an American. We seemed all ready to go to war against Iraq and fight terrorism as one nation.

After a couple of years of traveling, I missed Tyler a lot. It felt like we were growing farther and farther apart. I made lots of new friends at Philip Morris. Many individuals in upper management supported me in whatever I wanted to do, but all I wanted was to stop traveling. I figured if I went back to school, then some of the traveling would have to subside – especially if they were financing the education. So, I decided to go to law school. That's what I was preparing to do before Glen and I became roommates. I spoke to my Senior Director and told him my plans. I reported to him and the Vice President of Sales. Both of them were fond of me, respected my work ethics, and were ready to support me. The problem then was, I'd have to move to New York and work in the Legal department in order for them to finance the law degree.

When I talked to Tyler about it, he was against it. He said, "Why do we need two attorneys? Baby, I work a lot of hours already, and if you become an attorney, you think things are bad now because you're traveling, but it will be worse if you have to live in New York. Then when you finish law school, your schedule will be so demanding, just as mine is, we'd never be able to spend time together."

I was frustrated, I loved him but I really needed to stop traveling. I felt we could survive a long distance relationship. With my traveling schedule, it was like we were in one anyway. There was something else bothering me as well. So I told him, "I don't see where we are going with this relationship. In the past, I didn't want to be married, but now I do. If you don't want to marry me, then I just as well should leave."

"Baby, why would you say that? I don't want you to leave. I love you." He said while gazing into my eyes. "Why don't you go to graduate school here in California and get an MBA. When you finish, we'll get married and have a family."

"Really!" I said. "Okay, I'll do it." Well, I never wanted an MBA, but I went anyway, because I loved him and was ready to settle down and get married. So, back to school I went while still tirelessly working at Philip Morris.

One day in early 2003, I received a call from Paul about their aunt, Ann. "Treesa, you need to go see about Ann. She hit her head and she's in the hospital." I wasn't sure why he was calling me. I was still the person no one could trust – the thief. I hadn't heard from him in so long, and he called me as if we had just spoken last week.

"What? Well, what happened?" I asked.

"I don't know, she fell and hit her head. You need to go and see about her." Paul said. He told me she was in Huntington Memorial.

I hung up and called the hospital. The nurse said, "Thank good-ness someone called. We have been trying to get in touch with someone from her family. Your aunt had a brain aneurysm and we need to do surgery. She will probably need a blood transfusion as well. Can you come to the hospital to sign the consent form?" I told her I would be there as soon as I could. I immediately called Paul back and informed him of my conversation with the nurse. I told him that Ann had a brain aneurysm and needed surgery; and that he needed to meet me at the hospital.

When I arrived at the hospital, I saw Paul's wife instead of him. I went directly to the nurse's station to inquire about Ann. Paul's wife spotted me talking to one of the nurses at the desk, walked up to me and said, "What are you doing here?" while twisting her face up at me as if I smelled. I was still considered the black sheep or the outcast of the family over the whole money thing. But, I was also the one that most of them would call if they were in need.

I threw my hands up. "I don't have time for you," I snapped back. By then the doctor had walked over to us. He explained Ann's dire situation and I explained that Paul was a Jehovah's Witness and did not support the use of blood transfusions to sustain life. He had recently been baptized into the faith. He asked if I would sign the consent, and I said, "Of course, she would want to live." Then I explained that I was not a blood niece. By then, Paul showed up. The doctor asked if he would sign the consent. He said "No, let nature take its course."

The doctor asked if she had any children. I said "No". He explained that legally, since there was no immediate blood relative, in these cases, the doctor could sign for her, and so he did. Although Ann was the same woman who had spread nasty incestuous rumors about me and Glen, she still had the right to live.

In the end, Ann pulled through and was sent to a convalescent home. Her neighbor and I visited her daily. We would bring her food, shower gels, pajamas, clean her and thoroughly wash her feet – in between her toes. You know, when those people in the convalescent homes clean the patients, they do not get in the nooks and crannies very well. So we made sure Ann was well kept. She was never the same though. She suffered from Grand mal seizures and other medical problems, so I would always do what I could to help her. Most of the time, she just called me when she needed money, but we became close.

As the years went by, I think the only thing that got me through the long days of working and long nights of studying, was the promise from Tyler that we'd get married after I completed graduate school. Our relationship was strong and we were on the same page. About six months prior to graduation, I found out I was pregnant. I was very excited, not that we had planned to get pregnant before marriage, but it happened and I was thrilled.

After the second month into the pregnancy, I went over to visit one evening. While we were lying in each other's arms discussing plans for our lives, Tyler said, "I know I promised we'd get married and have a life together, but while you've been attending graduate school," He paused and I turned and stared directly into his eyes as he finished telling me, "things have changed for me. I no longer want to get married. There are a lot of complex issues that I hadn't discussed with you before and I really don't want to talk about them."

Tears flooded my eyes. I couldn't believe what I was hearing. This man that I had loved for years, the man whose child I was carrying, just told me without an ounce of compassion that he changed his mind, just as if he was telling me he changed dinner plans.

"What are you saying?" I asked, but already knew.

He started in his legal tone as if he were giving a summation to the jurors for the client he just so eloquently represented. I didn't wait to hear anything else. I grabbed my clothes and left.

A few months after Tyler told me he no longer wanted to marry me, I graduated with my MBA and shortly afterward, gave birth to my son, Jaydon, who is the love of my life. His father, a man I loved, admired, and respected for nearly a decade was out of my life without much of an explanation. Pain and rejection seemed to always be a constant in my life. Now, I was getting too old to weather the pain of rejection and heartbreak; I was breaking down physically and emotionally. Being a new mother, I knew I couldn't continue the work pace expected at Philip Morris – and I didn't want to. I wanted a life. I wanted to spend all my time with my fat, bouncy, baby boy.

Regardless of how much I wanted to leave Philip Morris to settle down with my son, once again I was alone. Now, I had to feed and take care of my son, I wanted to give him the best that life had to offer. From time to time, I looked for jobs that would pay me comparable to the salary I received at Philip Morris but would also give me more quality time to spend with Jaydon. It seemed nothing was out there for me, so I continued the brutal pace. However, the travel decreased some.

In 2004, President Bush won the election for his second term, but only by a hair. In my opinion, he exploited the September 11 attacks to instill fear in people as a scare tactic to win the election.

Then, when Bush announced that the new Secretary of State would be Condoleeza Rice, an African-American woman, I wondered whether it was just another ploy to calm down the black community. But even with my skepticism of him, I was so proud to see an African-American woman hold such a high position. We were moving on up. I believed the Republicans were beginning to realize that the black community was paying attention more to politics so they were trying to connect with us to capture our votes. That seemed to be a great task for them since they had given us little regard in the past.

This proved to be a good decision for Bush, helping to provide the correct fibers to bind and weave us together as a mighty nation. We were smack dab in the middle of a terrorist war which again he played on throughout his campaign.

It took three years before I was able to resign from Philip Morris and accept a contracted position in the health care industry as a Project Manager in the training department. I absolutely loved my two new managers. They were very empathetic to my situation-being a single mother. It seemed they were able to see the stress in my face and look through my eyes and see that I had been beaten up both physically, mentally, and emotionally. Though I remained a very private person and hadn't told my story to anyone, I believe it was my outward appearance that spoke to them loudly and clearly.

One evening, I was sitting on my son's bed with him in my lap, reading him a bedtime story. When I finished, I looked down at him and told him how blessed I was to have him.

He looked me directly in my eyes, and said, "I know Mommy, that's why God sent me here to be with you, so you wouldn't be alone anymore."

I was a little shocked and replied, "Who sent you here?" I knew he could not have really said what I thought he said, because although kids have great imaginations, I would think he wouldn't have these kinds of imaginations because, since leaving the religion I was raised in, I wasn't a member of any church. As a matter of fact, I hadn't even really visited any churches, except once when I was invited to a Resurrection Service with my friend, Jacques. So I thought, *where in the world did he get this idea from?*

Looking at me with such big innocent eyes, he said, "Oh, God did, Mommy."

"When did he tell you that?" I asked.

"When I use to live with him up in the heavens." He said as he nuzzled his head into my chest and closed his eyes.

Chapter Fourteen
Glen and I Reunited

It was summer of 2008 and I was living in Altadena. One day, there was a knock at my door. I opened it and there stood my cousin, Glen. As always, his eyes told the story before he could even open his mouth. This was the first time I had seen him since my Grandpa Mac died, about six years ago. He had called me before coming and said we needed to talk.

"Hey Cous."

"Hi Glen. Come on in." I pushed the door open for him to enter. Since he had never been to my new home, I guided him to the family room. I offered him something to drink, but he refused. As he sat down on the couch, his eyes were telling me he was sorry, but I needed to hear it from his mouth.

He told me that he had decided to do the Dr. Drew show and he wanted my support. At the time, I didn't even think about why it was my support he wanted. I just felt angry. Here he was asking me for something. The memory of past events began to monopolize my every thought. The pain and the betrayal I thought I had mentally escaped rushed back. Tiny electrical shocks struck my arms, upper chest and the back of my neck. I couldn't believe how quickly these feelings flooded me. So, of course, before I would agree to do what he asked, I had to let him have it. Even with the pain he caused me, he knew in his heart I would always be there for him because he's my little cousin and I loved him dearly. So I sat there and I scolded him for what he had done to me and for allowing the family to make such nasty, despicable comments, because he knew the truth. Glen apologized. I told him that I would support him, but I would, by no means, participate in the taping of the show; and I didn't.

Time went on and we became close again. Glen enjoyed spending time with Jaydon. They'd go fishing, play basketball, ride skateboards – all the things boys do. We pretty much patched things up from the past, but every so often, a little tinge of anger crept in.

I try to keep in mind a sermon on forgiveness Bishop Noel Jones delivered when I visited his church back in 2000. He said something like, "if you really forgive someone, then that means you can turn the clock back, and resume the relationship from the point before the offense occurred." I would work on that with my cousin.

One day, I received a call from Ann. I hadn't heard from her in a while, so I was concerned. I asked, "Are you okay? Do you need some money?"

"No baby, I don't need anything, I'm getting food from the food bank now and it's more than enough. I was just thinking about you and I wondered if I ever thanked you for all you did for me when I was sick? You know my memory is bad with these seizures and things, Baby. You know back then I didn't really have anybody, but you took care of me and I couldn't remember if I ever thanked you."

I was so surprised because she kept calling me "Baby". Ann was never the sweet or mushy type. She was more of a big, burly, bully of a woman. I said, "Yes Ann, you thanked me." We chatted a little more before hanging up. I sat down and thought how life can have a way of changing people. About a month later, Ann passed away.

In fact, the whole nation was changing. Barack Hussein Obama had won the primary election and now was predicted to be the first African-American President of the United States of America. He wasn't a descendant of a slave, like most of us. He was born to a free, Ivy League-educated, African man and a well-educated white woman who seemed to just love people for who they were and what they stood for. That was the impression I got from Obama's books.

He and I were born on the same day, August 4th. Just before the 2008 elections, I went to urgent care at Kaiser, the health care network, to have blood drawn. The nurse noticed my birth date in the charts and said in her broken English, "Oh, you have the most lucky birth date. You're August 4th like the candidate, Barack Obama. Are you going to vote for him?" she asked, not realizing that who a person votes for is usually a private issue. But I replied.

"Yes." I hadn't been sure during the months prior, but my son Jaydon followed the primaries and told me this man would be elected as our president.

The nurse said you must vote for him. A lot of my friends and I (they were of Asian decent) have studied the various Asian and American numerology, astrology, and readings. They all say, "He was born to be a king! This is his inherited birth right. He was sent from God to take his rightful position in life. For that reason, my friends and I will vote for him, even though we are Republican." The talkative nurse went on to say, "You have this same lucky birth date, just a different year. The year makes a difference in Chinese astrology, but the month and day are important in other readings. You must find your purpose, you are destined for greatness." I wondered, *Am I at the hospital or at a fortune teller's office?* Then I thought, *If she only knew my story….At this point, all I wanted to do was survive.*

November 4, 2008. It was time for America to cast her votes. I took Jaydon with me to the poll to experience this historical moment. Even at the young age of four, he could hold an intelligent conversation about the election. I was impressed with his excitement over the race for the presidency, and since he had followed the primaries from the beginning and predicted that Barack Obama would win, I allowed him to cast the vote for our future president, Mr. Obama.

That night, like millions of other Americans, Jaydon and I watched the news intensely. It was finally announced that Obama had won and was now the 44th President of the United States. I began to cry like many others. Black, white, Korean, Latino, and all ethnicities were moved by the victory which projected a new message throughout the world – a message bigger than the confined walls of America. This election told the world that people of color had value.

I remembered the faces of young black men and women in the 90s, with the deep darkness in their eyes as they torched America, yelling "No Justice! No Peace!" I knew at this moment, a change had truly come. Not just because Obama had said so, but because a new generation had stood up to America with the power of their votes. Although the actions of many of the young people from the LA riots were misguided, the world was forced to take notice. Contrary to popular belief, many of the protestors were willing and ready to sacrifice their freedom to fight for equality and justice as the marchers and Dr. King had done in the sixties. Media would like for us to just focus on the looters, but within the LA riots was an uprising of good people who began the demonstrations at the Parker Center. Tempers flared and this planned peaceful demonstration soon got out of control; but the intent of these people of all races was to simply announce, "This was not okay and we were not taking it anymore." Dr. King may have grimaced at their actions, but they got the job done. The message would be heard throughout the world. No Justice! No Peace!

As I reflect on my life, it seems like yesterday when I was just a little tomboy racing around the block, wrestling, playing football, and hooking worms or sardines to a fishing hook – all for the sake of keeping up with Dwayne, Gailyn, Morgan, and Glen. Thank God for gymnastics! It was my only saving grace into young lady hood. The time I spent growing up with all of my cousins remains very special to me. It was the only time I got a chance to be a child, let my nappy hair down, and be free of a big sister's responsibilities. As each of my male cousins challenged me to make sure I could do all the things that they could do, my position in all of their hearts was sealed to me. We were all brothers back then, until I turned eleven and I realized they had become stronger that me. Then, I had to be the sister.

As our life experiences continue, here we stand as adults, immersed and suffocating in heartbreak from the death of our loved ones, the break-up of our marriages and relationships, the disappointment of our friends and family members. Most detrimental of all, guaranteed to stop you dead in your tracks, is the haunting ghost of fear that lingers from rejection and discrimination. Through it all, you should always be able to depend and count on family for support. That's just how we were raised. No matter what, at the end, be there for one another.

I never imagined my life would be filled with so many enriching, historic experiences, events, and memories – mostly, because Glen chose me, of all of our cousins, to walk with him in his journey of divine order. That's what I call it, divine order. The way I see it, he had no control over the historic event of March 3, 1991 – not even the mere fact that his very vessel was selected because its strength could withstand the depraved, brutal, violent beating of his attackers. Nor did those officers realize they were coming to work that day to become suspects of such a vile, criminal act orchestrated by their own hands. No, the stage of that scene, I'm sure, was written and set way before any of us were conceived.

I stumble, fall, and sometimes bleed a bit, but that's all part of the journey to success. It is important that we walk in courage and faith, and disallow the fear from our injuries to malign our emotions and confidence. It is the power of fear that prevents us from moving forward and robs us of our true inherited gift from our heavenly father. As we experience life, the people we think we need the most, or should be there to support us when we fall, either cannot or will not; but you can still live with that. That moment is truly the time to celebrate your very existence on earth and to thank the heavenly father for your own inception; embracing pain and conflict from experiences so that you may become wiser and properly equipped for the remainder of your journey. That's what I've done in my life.

Today, I celebrate my life as a successful mother, and a public access talk show host. The show is called "The Color of Success." It symbolizes the color of the essence you leave behind as you travel through life. It has given me a forum to inspire, motivate, showcase, and celebrate culture, creativity, and success of ordinary people in our community in order to build cohesion and a passion to live, love, and inspire each other, in spite of our differences. www.TheColor-of-Success.com

Glen came over two weeks ago to remind me about the twentieth anniversary of the riots. MTV and VH1 wanted interviews. They were interested in hearing about the Stranded Project because of its place in history. They thought other people who never got the opportunity would like to hear it also.

The conversation we had that day made me contemplate what we had endured and how much I had grown from these experiences. I felt an obligation to teach and tell our story in my own way for a change. Therefore, I decided to chronicle these events, because I think we - all ethnicities – learned so much from the events of March 3, 1991 and April 29, 1992.

Final Words

I am a descendent of a humble, yet strong group of people who were sacrificial lambs, and have carried what seemed to be the cross of Jesus Christ for over four centuries. They were sold and stolen from their homeland and held captive, waiting to board the next human cargo ship in the Trans-Atlantic and Triangular slave trade. During the voyage, they were packed and stacked on top of each other without adequate breathing room and food to eat – chained together, forcing human feces to drain onto their faces and bodies and infecting them with incurable diseases. Millions were thrown into the Atlantic Ocean to discard the stench of death before reaching America. No one really knows the exact number. For hundreds of years, there was improper documentation and some-times none at all, accounting for the Africans who were taken and lost their lives during the slave trade. But, it is estimated that over 20 million Africans were transported to America, and millions of them never made it. This is probably, the greatest understated atrocity in the history of human civilization. It is referred to as the African or Black Holocaust. My ancestors were brought to America as slaves to cultivate and farm the land, work with metals, design and build cities and infrastructure. This great country where we all reside, and enjoy its beauty and luxuries – was built by Africans who were not even considered human beings at the time.

Twenty years ago the L.A. riots represented the pain, suffering, and frustration of African-American people who suffered at the hands of the unjust, and displaced in the economic system of the greatest country in the world, built on the backs of our great-grandparents while everyone else prospered and enjoyed the fruit of our labor. That's what it felt like.

While there is no justification for the violent mayhem committed on 4/29/92, it should be a day of remembrance and reflection on the pain we caused to our fellow neighbors because of injustice, cultural indifferences and intolerance. It is an event in our history that we must all atone for, and never allow to happen again. My new friend, Tina, says, "America is not a melting pot; instead, it is a huge salad with many different fruits that coexist, and that's what makes America the beautiful country it is. If we take time to expose our cultures to each other and embrace the differences, we'll all evolve and learn from each other.

From Michele

When I was approached by Ontresicia Averette to write her story, first, I was honored that she entrusted me with this task. Secondly, the more we discussed it and the direction in which she wanted it to go, I was impressed with her enthusiasm to have her story become a teaching tool to instruct all races of how intolerance, discrimination, and disrespect of others can negatively impact our society as a whole.

As I began my research and interview process of the people impacted by the 1992 LA riots (Koreans, Hispanics, blacks, and whites), I was both enlightened and sadden by the stories I heard. I was often reminded of this quote, *"People fail to get along because they fear each other; they fear each other because they don't know each other; they don't know each other because they have not communicated with each other,"* said Martin Luther King, Jr.

I would like to thank everyone that participated and assisted me with this project. Special thanks to Karen Shaw for helping me pull it all together. Julie Ha, for always responding to every one of my questions in detail regarding the impact the L.A. riots had on the Korean-American community; and who also introduced me to the Children of Sa-i-gu. Last, but definitely not least, the interviewees, Joseph Fennell, Kellie Davies, Richard Kim, and Geoffrey Gill, who shared their personal experiences and thoughts on the riots.

In our efforts to give all ethnic groups a voice in this book and to bring all races some knowledge of how the other felt during this calamity, we've added those interviews shared by the people mentioned above, who were impacted by the 1992 L.A. riots, beginning with the Children of Sa-i-gu.

Interviews

Children of Sa-i-gu

Sa-i-gu translates as "4-29," and is understood by Korean-speaking people to mean the Los Angeles riots of 1992, and follows the Korean convention of referring to historic events, both watershed and cataclysmic, by their numerical dates.

The following interviews are from KoreAm Journal, April, 2002 from the perspective of the children of Korean immigrants by K.W. Lee, a veteran Korean American journalist. Special thanks to Julie Ha.

PETER CHO was a happy-go-lucky fifth-grader until Sa-i-gu hit and rioters destroyed his mother's Koreatown store.

He and his sisters watched on TV as the store, which sold women's clothing at Vermont Ave. and Eighth St., turned to burnt rubble. Only 11 at the time, he felt helpless. It was hard to bear his mother's seemingly unending tears. Now a student at UC Riverside, he says he has yet to talk with his mother about Sa-i-gu, but that's a conversation the 21-year-old is determined to have.

Before I could really say anything, I heard the garage door open. It was my parents, both in their own cars, which were packed to the top with merchandise from the store. As soon as they walked into the house, my mother saw her store in ruins on TV. She had left her store just before the looting had begun in that part of Korea town. My mother burst into tears. She had put her past five-plus years into that store, and she was just about to sell it when this happened.

I thought many things in my head: Why did those Mexicans and black people have to burn my mom's store? She didn't do anything to them. She was just trying to support her family.

Mothers and sons have a special bond, and I never really felt it until that day. It was as if my mother's pain became mine. If anything had happened to my mother, I think I would have gone crazy and tried something crazy like shoot at [the rioters] with a gun. But then again, what good would that have done?

I just wanted my mother to stop crying. Sometimes, she would smile with tears in her eyes and tell me, "Everything will be all right, Petey." It was a momentary feeling of how everything was going to work out for our family, but I knew it wasn't going to be easy.

May 1st, was when I got to see in person what was once my mother's store. It was a black pile of wood, glass and metal. I thought we were going to stay at the store, but we headed over to a Korean radio station where they were giving out food for the riot victims. I thought to myself, "Why are we going here?" I never thought my family had to resort to this. Were we poor now? I felt like crying, but the last thing I wanted to do was make my mother cry, too. So I held in those tears.

I was hurt because of my family's situation, but also sad because all these people who were standing in line for aid packages of food and other items were going through the same thing. I was sad that a part of Korea town died a couple of days earlier. All the mom-and-pop stores that were once proudly decorating the district of Korea town were gone. Things got worse for my family. We lost our house in Walnut. We ended up moving three times in the next five years.

JENNY AN, UC San Diego student who grew up in Korea town, was 10 during Sa-i-gu. She attended Wilton Place Elementary School, and in her particular class, she was the only Korean among primarily black and Latino students.

On the first day of the Riots, she remembers hysteria at school and feeling scared she was going to die. A few days later, she didn't want to return to school, but her mother insisted on it.

At school, I remember this Mexican kid came up to me and said, "You, stupid Korean." He's like, "I hate you."

I just started crying. I said, "What are you talking about?" He said, "Because of you, everything is ruined." I said, "You guys are the ones who were stealing everything, you guys were robbing everyone." I was crying and going off on him.

One black kid comes and he goes, "Well, you know, you Koreans hate all black people." I said, "I don't hate black people. I don't hate you."

He said, "Yeah, you do."

And that's when I totally realized what racism was. I didn't even know what prejudice was before then.

JUNE LIM, a 13-year-old was too young to process exactly what Sa-i-gu meant to her and other Korean Americans. Now a youth counselor at the Korean Youth and Community Center, she is retracing those memories.

Although the fires and looting didn't reach her family's Gardena liquor store, she says her weeping mother couldn't help but imagine that the burning stores on TV could have been theirs. She also remembers well her father's decision not to arm himself with a gun to protect the family business.

I recall two of my uncles coming to my father's store at night to defend it just in case. Another thing that sharply sticks in my mind is that even though the situation was potentially dangerous, my father stuck to his morals about not arming himself with a gun. My uncle had borrowed one from his friend, but my father refused to use it. Instead, he depended on brooms and my brother's street hockey sticks for protection. I will forever respect my father for his decision. My father and uncles would spend the night at the store in the days following the Riots. My father told me about how his customers would come by and check up on him. Some would even make visits at night, saying they were there to protect the store. Many of the black and Latino customers would call a couple of times during the day to make sure that everything was OK. These are the stories that go untold in everyday media.

I hope that Korean Americans, especially second-generation, can learn from and understand Sa-i-gu. We really need to foster a sense of community and ownership of our community. We have to learn to work together, with other Asian Americans and, furthermore, with other people of color. We need to understand that the world does not turn from the self-centered I/me perspective, but the way we can survive and thrive in America is from the inclusive us/we point of view.

Interview with Joseph F. Fennell Jr

Then - Narcotics Detective, Los Angeles Sheriff's Department
Now Commander - Custody Division, Los Angeles Sheriff's Department

MW: One of the things that have always bothered me is that the police didn't step in and stop the violence being thrashed upon the innocent people of L.A. Why didn't the police help? People were getting slaughtered out there.

JF: LAPD helped a lot of people. We (police officers) were prepared for isolated incidents and the police were well trained to handle such situations. The majority of law enforcement agencies have a cadre of personnel on stand-by to handle these types of isolated incidents, but when the South Central area basically "blew up," starting with the Reginald Denny situation …It became increasingly challenging to try and control the magnitude of people rushing on the streets creating havoc and violence.

MW: OK. Earlier you told me they (the police) had to retreat for their own safety. Can you explain?

JF: We as law enforcement officers mirror the same character traits as the rest of society. You have to remember that the police come from the same cloth as everybody else, the only thing that differentiates us from others is that we put on this uniform and we're well trained in police science and law enforcement tactics. We are trained to handle violent situations, situations that are uncomfortable for most people. Police officers will place their life in danger in an effort to save the life of a person who is unknown to them. Fortunately for the citizens of Los Angeles, LAPD and LASD are among the most highly trained law enforcement organizations in the nation. Both agencies spend tremendous time and money training their personnel and exploring innovative training techniques. As a result of that training, both organizations, handled the LA riots quite well, however, both organizations learned their weakness from the volumes of incidents which occurred. Because of the friction between the African American community and law enforcement surrounding the Rodney King situation, the two entities were extremely divided. One of the best actions that LAPD implemented was retreating because they were not equipped to handle the magnitude of all the people which flowed onto the streets of Los Angeles. At the time, that was the best decision they could have made.

MW: Yes, because I kept seeing and hearing LAPD only and I thought well what about our Sheriff's Department?

JF: LAPD is a very proud organization and at the time their Chief (Darryl Gates) felt they could handle the situation without the assistance of other law enforcement agencies. LAPD could have immediately requested Mutual Aid, which would have activated the County Emergency System and provided additional law enforcement resources from agencies throughout Los Angeles County. But I don't believe anyone in the law enforcement arena could have predicted that the situation would evolve to the magnitude of a riot. Therefore, I believe LAPD's command staff's initial assessment of the situation was valid. They felt as an organization they possessed the necessary internal personnel resources to handle the various events, therefore

LAPD's request for Mutual Aid was delayed. Once Mutual Aid was requested, there are numerous components of emergency management which must be taken into consideration such as, but not limited to tactical planning; the utilization of additional personnel and resources; communications, how are the various law enforcement agencies going to communicate. This is due to the fact that every police department has different frequencies. Interoperability was a major obstacle. There are a multitude of factors to consider, including but not limited to the types of weapons being used, vehicles, commissary for on-duty personnel, relief for the personnel, etc.... As far as tactical planning is concern when a crowd is dispersed, which direction should law enforcement personnel direct the crowd; is the crowd being dispersed back into the neighborhood? Is the crowd being dispersed near a freeway on-ramp? What's our goal? How will these decisions impact the safety of the neighborhood going forward? Traffic issues must be considered. There is an abundance of tactical planning occurring simultaneously to any large scale event, especially a riot. LAPD's decision to regroup and further assess the sequence of events was a sound decision. It may have been unsettling for people to understand because people in multiple communities were expressing their frustrations on other people and businesses. Unfortunately people were injured. However, law enforcement could not intercede without implementing a strategy to rescue injured citizens and protect businesses. If a person was being assaulted, let's use the Reginald Denny incident, where he was being pulled out of his car. It's difficult to digest, however, sufficient law enforcement personnel is necessary to combat the crowd and safely rescue Mr. Denny. If several law enforcement officers react to the situation without a plan and take independent action in an effort to rescue Mr. Denny, then they become part of the problem and not the solution. What I mean is that without a strategy, the individual officers would not know the plan their fellow officers are trying to accomplish therefore, each officer is operating on an individual mindset which could subject them to requesting rescue. That is why it is important for officers to respond in an organized fashion. Officers must develop a strategy to disperse the crowd and rescue Mr. Denny. Then avail Mr. Denny to the services of the Fire Department and paramedics at a safe location. Law enforcement personnel have to think about all of these factors. There are a lot of moving parts, all moving simultaneously.

MW: OK, I get that now, thanks for clearing it up. Where were you when the riots began? Were you watching the riots from the station?

JF: At the time I was a Senior Narcotics Investigator. I was working on a narcotics case with my partners in the South Bay area. We heard about the rioting. However, we did not understand or know the magnitude of the situation. We thought they were isolated incidents. Once we returned to our office, we huddled around a television with other officers, and saw the destruction which was occurring. Buildings being set on fire, people breaking into stores taking merchandise, and everything associated with a riot. We could not believe this was happening in Los Angeles. We waited, expecting to be called out as part of an emergency response. There was talk of putting on our uniforms and driving to the area to offer our assistance. But smarter minds prevailed and we awaited direction from our supervisors.

MW: Let's go back for a minute. So how did you feel as a black man watching the videotape of Rodney King being beat by law enforcement?

JF: Look, I worked patrol in South Central Los Angeles during the mid-eighties when crack cocaine was an epidemic on the streets of Los Angeles. I have witnessed unusual violence in the neighborhoods we patrolled including being involved in episodes of necessary force with the criminal element. I clearly understand the use of force, it is associated with our profession. In the case of Rodney King everyone had a different opinion or emotion because he was a black man being beaten by Caucasian police officers in a way that to me was unsettling. By viewing the videotapes that was shown to the public, it's my personal opinion that the amount of force used was not in-line with their department's policy. Of course, as a black man, I felt hurt and it took me aback. When I saw the way the officers responded or should I say, their lack of ownership to the incident, I felt they didn't represent the law enforcement community.

MW: How did you feel when you saw the explosion? The Riots?

JF: What happened to Rodney King was unacceptable, but society should not respond with violence because that's not going to resolve the issues. There has to be an intelligent format where we can engage in open, meaningful dialogue. It's incumbent for us to gather all the major stakeholders and form constructive working groups with a common goal to enhance the relationships between the African American community and local law enforcement. The dialogue should address concerns and problems in our past and how we can resolve these issues going forward. I realize there is a lot of internal anger towards law enforcement. I believe Town Hall meetings are an excellent forum to have open dialogue and accomplish this mission. When I witnessed minorities, I'm talking about African Americans and Hispanics, acting in such a violent, retaliatory way towards each other and another ethnic group – it sickened me. Several of my Caucasian co-workers were displeased by how the officers in the Rodney King situation conducted themselves. The officers involved in Rodney King case did not represent the law enforcement community, nevertheless, I believe people over-reacted, and took advantage of the circumstances for their own selfish reasons.

MW: You say they blew it out of proportion but did you sort of understand that rage because it wasn't just about Rodney King, it was about other injustices towards blacks that were still in their psyche? LaTasha Harlins had been shot in the back of the head just 13 days after Rodney King had been beaten. That was on the minds of a lot of people because I know every time I saw her face on the news it reminded me of Nikki's (my daughter) school picture. That woman didn't do one day of jail time. The black community was feeling like their lives had no value at all. Don Jackson had proven that the police in certain areas targeted black men. So could you understand their rage although clearly their actions were wrong?

JF: I understand, but these were isolated incidents where the African American communities felt they were dealt injustices. It appeared the community felt powerless. I get that, but in our history as African Americans we have been subjected to a host of injustices. The Latasha Harlins case, it's a sad, unfortunate incident which should've never happened. However, we can't bring her back, and by African Americans reacting in a violent manner only inflamed the situation. Innocent citizens suffered harm, because of the actions of a few incorrigible characters. We as African Americans are smarter than that; we're educated and hopefully learned from our past. The Don Jackson situation was totally different. According to the law enforcement debriefing, I received Don Jackson as an agitator. He was a former police officer, who was familiar with police tactics. He knew what to say and do to cause a reaction from police officers. He instigated that whole incident. He had a detail strategy, which worked. He chose the location and he chose the method in the way in which it was going to happen. He was uncooperative and used enough resistance, not a lot, for the police officer to find it necessary to implement a force component. He continued his resistances which cause the police officer to respond with additional resistance. They engaged in basically a pushing and shoving scenario where Mr. Jackson ended up falling through a window. Mr. Jackson carried out his strategy to perfection.

MW: OK but I can't set you up to do something if it's not something that you're not going to do. That's like saying – I'm going to plant some money somewhere to get you to steal it. If it's not your nature… no matter how hard I try to entice you with this money or equipment or whatever, it's not going to happen. What can I say to you as an officer that's going to make you want to push my head into a window?

JF: You have to peel back the onion a little bit. He knew if he conducted himself in a certain manner and verbalized certain words, the police officer would react in an aggressive way. Based upon what I have been told about the incident he targeted Long Beach Police Department.

MW: So then he (Don Jackson) proved his point because they were aggressive officers.

JF: He proved a point to an extent, but we don't know what was said prior to the videotaping. We don't know what scenario took place prior to the actual events that were captured on videotape. Of course, I'm giving some latitude towards the officers, based upon information I was told. That being said, we all should use caution before arriving at a definite opinion, unless we know all the facts of the case. We're all guilty of pre-judging without having intricate knowledge of the situations. Honestly, I can't intelligently evaluate any of the aforementioned situations without having investigative knowledge of each situation, however, like the majority of society, we obtain limited information via various sources, then form opinions.

MW: OK I see but what I'm saying is whatever I say to an officer – those are just words I don't care if I curse at an officer, those are just words. You should be able to handle it and resist, as an officer, from your training to take whatever words I spew out. Now when I strike you then you have every right to beat my butt, but if I'm just saying words I shouldn't be able to incite you to do whatever I want you to do…an officer should have more control than that.

JF: I agree, but as I said from the start, police are cut from the same human cloth….we come out of the same population census. Our parents are civilians, our siblings are civilians, and our friends are civilians. Back to Rodney King – allow me to provide some personal insight. I believe, in my mind, we (African American law enforcement detectives) played a prominent role for our respective departments. Once LAPD requested mutual aid, then our department decided to use African American detectives in an undercover capacity, to gain intelligence. We meshed with the crowd and obtained insightful intelligence. As the day progressed people started sharing information with us pertaining to the location of meetings. Some meetings were being held to incite the riot. Instigators were meeting at various locations…they were organized.

MW: Are you serious. This was organized?

JF: Yes. We met in open parking lots, community buildings, at times at churches. I'm sure when we met at churches it was without the Pastors or the congregations knowledge or involvement. The leaders would huddle in the rear of the church, away from the congregation and formalized riotous activities. They scheduled their activities each day, sometimes by the hour…especially the gang members. We went to those meetings to gain an understanding of their plans and strategies. We took that information to our Command staff, who informed the officers working the field. Of course, the rioters had a feeling that undercover police officers were among the population. The leaders of these meetings would always say make sure you check everybody coming in and out of these places, yet no one ever did. Occasionally they would make some type of threatening statement, such as "if we find out you're a police officer we're going to kill you." I believe a few of the hard core gang members would have used this opportunity to harm or kill a police officer. Especially if they were surrounded by other people who shared their mentality or succumb to the mob mentality. It was dangerous for us, and I believe all the undercover officers shared some level of fear. We possessed our firearms and were prepared to use them if necessary. Truly by us integrating ourselves into that rioter's mob mentality we were able to ascertain a lot of information, especially the strategic locations that different organized gangs were going to destroy. As I mentioned earlier, we would inform our Command Staff, who would disseminate this information to the field officers, who would establish a safe perimeter around those selected locations. At some locations 24 hour surveillance for a few days was necessary to ensure that those different historic establishments would not be burned down or destroyed.

MW: That's very interesting. I didn't know it was that deep with the rioters.

Rodney King really wanted his music project to be positive and to serve as a deterrent against police brutality but when he said can we all get along some people were angry. Especially young people. What did you think about that statement?

JF: Based upon interviews of Rodney King, he did not portray himself as a violent person. People took this as an opportunity to vent their personal anger. This had little to do with Rodney King; it had everything to do with people using this event as a tool to vent their anger. Rodney King was an instrument for people to rally around and cause havoc and violence on the city of LA….and that's what occurred.

MW: He certainly didn't want to see this happen….as a matter a fact when an attorney got Damien Williams' off with a much lesser charge than he deserved by saying it wasn't his fault. Everybody or rather a lot of people were happy but King told his cousin Ontresicia that made him sick. "That man (Reginald Denny) didn't deserve that. We weren't raised like that." Remember in his press conference, he said, "think about the older people and children."

JF: We associate the riots to the Rodney King incident. However, I don't think Rodney King would ever endorse the actions of the rioters. As previously stated, people used this as an instrument to vent their racial tension. I witnessed African American teenagers, as young as 10 years old in the streets late at night, involved in criminal activity. These children had limited knowledge, if any of the incident involving Rodney King, but were influenced by other young adults. I questioned if some of them even understood the historical struggles of African Americans. Truly, I was disappointed by their actions. Our forefathers, trail blazed for African Americans, to obtain a better quality of life, which included education , in order for us to become a productive part of society. Change the direction of our future and place us on equal footing. Our ancestors literally fought for jobs; however, I'm witnessing kids in the riot trying to burn down the city and was unable to explain why they are rioting. Many of the older adults, especially the women were telling the rioters "You guys shouldn't do this…Baby don't do this….baby you guys not acting right…baby go home…" The elderly adults tried to impart knowledge and wisdom. Nevertheless, many of the rioters were caught in the "mob mentality." I equate it to sand at the beach. As the grains of sand blows in the direction of the strongest wind, back and forth, that's how the rioters acted they blew in the direction of the strongest voice. They thought it was fun. There were people conducting themselves in such unethical way, they would have never acted in that manner if they were alone.

MW: You know what you just said? You just basically said the same thing the attorney said to get Damien Williams crime reduced... it was true.

He (Faal) used the The Riot Frenzy Theory – how individuals in a group can act together without planned direction.

JF: Well, Los Angeles experienced and validated his theory. I'm sure this riot was the foundation of an assortment of case studies from a host of scholars on human behavior theorems. Illustrated is the fact that the majority of us, in society, are followers. We conduct ourselves according to how society expects us to act or from learned behavior.

MW: Well that's very interesting. You have been very insightful and have given the readers something else to think about. Thank you for taking the time out to do this interview. I really appreciate your time and thoughts on this subject.

Interview with Kellie Davies

Then – Project Manager, Cedars Sinai Medical Center
Now – Project Manager, Cedars Sinai Medical Center

MW: How did you feel when you saw Rodney King being beat?

KD: I watched very carefully. I must have watched it a dozen times. Rodney was a good size man you know but in my personal opinion they had enough cops where they could have handled it in a better way. Whether you want to say if he was on PCP or whatever, I understand the threat, but they really did do him wrong when they beat him up. To watch it and to deny it happened, is taking sides for the wrong reason. I heard a lot of people making excuses for them (the police). "They're cops, they're people of authority" or "they didn't really beat him" or "they didn't really do anything that bad." In my opinion, and you have to take every individual case and look at it honestly, they (the police) were wrong. But I was not surprised that jury ruled in favor of the police. Because 20 years ago they didn't have classes that taught the police appropriate behavior and proper use of force. Even though those courses are mandatory today, and things have changed to a degree, bad things still happen. There are some people that lose their temper quick and they should not be in law enforcement. But just watching this particular thing it was very obvious that it (the arrest of Rodney King) was out of control. It went rogue...it shouldn't have gone rogue. And anybody who's denying that is denying, what their eyes see....at least in my mind. I was surprised at the brutality of it, especially the blows to his head. It was really hard to watch because you're watching a human being, regardless of what he had done or had been accused of doing, they cracked him over the head. It was just hard to watch and they (the police) haven't got his side of the story yet. So that was my feeling from watching it. For me it was never about Rodney King being black and the cops being white or anything else. It was for me, right and wrong. To me you're innocent until proven guilty. And if he was a little forceful, they have stun guns, they have rubber bullets, etc. They (the police) had so many other options that would not cause permanent damage.

MW: So how did you feel when the verdicts came out? Not Guilty!

KD: Well first of all there was a lot of talk before the verdicts came out. I just heard people in general saying, "They're not going to get away with this. We're not going to stand for this anymore." You know, just overhearing comments from people I didn't even know. So I was already feeling tension. There was tension at work; there was just tension everywhere. People were glued to it pretty much like the OJ case. I was very afraid before I heard the verdicts that there was going to be big time tension between the black community and the police. I thought this can not possibly turn out good based on conversations I had over-heard, and what I was feeling in my gut. The tension was thick you could cut it with a knife. When I heard the verdict the first thing I thought, *"Oh hell, this is not good"*. I thought they were guilty and unfortunately, there are some people that can't change, and will never change, we can only change ourselves and how we think and feel. As far as I'm concerned, they should have gotten time. So I was surprised. I mean ….watch the tape people. But then again I think, if I remember correctly, weren't they pretty much tried in an all white area.

MW: Simi Valley.

KD: There you go. Some people in Simi Valley, and I don't mean everybody (So please don't personalize this), have an antiquated, red neck kind of view. So I recalled correctly, Simi Valley. I remember even before they went to trial and I found out it was going to be in this particular community I thought, this is not going to have a good outcome no matter how many times you showed them that tape. It's not going to have good outcome. If I was out in Simi Valley and the cops beat me up or something, I'd have no doubt that I would probably win just because I'm a white woman. If you sit on a jury and you're asked if you can be partial? I think a lot of people lie about that. I think a lot of people want to get on certain juries for the sensationalism, I think that they have already made up their mind before they even sit down. So I don't think Rodney King would have gotten justice there. Maybe if it (the trial) had been somewhere else, maybe in LA, where it's a little more diverse population. So I think those people just went in with their minds already made up.

MW: When the verdicts came out, where were you?

KD: I was at work. I was lucky because at that time I lived in West Hollywood so I was only about 10 minutes away from home. I was working the early shift so I was leaving around 3:30pm and I got home with no problems. However, I was dating a man that lived in Redondo Beach and I was supposed to drive down there for the weekend. When I got home, I had the TV on and was afraid. Later that evening, I watched people being pulled from cars. That one guy that was pulled from his truck.

MW: Reginald Denny.

KD: Yes. I couldn't believe what I was seeing, I felt like I was in a surreal moment. The main thought going through my head was, this is America. I understand that people get angry and I understand that you can't walk in another person's shoe, but as we were saying earlier, it's all in how you handle it. There's always going to be those people who are great in riling people up. They never seem to get into trouble; you know what I'm saying? I talked to Gary (my boyfriend) on the phone and I said, "Look, I'm not coming down there." Because to get to him I had to come straight down LaCienga to get on the 405 freeway or to take the 10 freeway to get the 405 freeway but at some point I had to take LaCienga and I was not going down that way. So Gary said he would come up and he did. He didn't encounter any problems but of course you know there was a heavy police presence where I was. When he got up to my place and we were watching the news, that's when it was getting dusk, there was a lot of mayhem going on then. There were two guys that were friends of mine that lived in a taller building across the street, so they told us to come over so we could see what was going on. Now this is in West Hollywood, this is what I mean about people inciting people…it just sort of spreads; it's like a bad infection that keeps spreading. We get up there on the balcony and you could see all of these spots of fires everywhere. We were standing there talking, all of a sudden people come walking by, there was some kind of electronic store around the corner (I think Silo or something), these people were walking up my street (I was just south of Sunset) with boxes of electronic equipment.

They were shouting, "hey go over and get some stuff", and they weren't black. These were white guys and Mexican guys with their girlfriends with them. People who looked like they belonged in West Hollywood, and I mean it was just people taking advantage of what was a terrible moment. I didn't go running around to the store to help myself with whatever was there. In my mind that's not how civilized people behave. There are rules and laws, we may not always like them, that we are suppose to live by in this country. I live by them. I'm very afraid to break the law. I respect it. Anyway, even today 20 years later, I was very very angry at the black people in the community. In their community where they live, they destroyed thier neighborhood stores, they destroyed the mom and pop stores, the liquor stores, the electronic stores, they burned things, they destroyed cars and the thing that really pissed me off was they did it in their own neighborhood. I got very angry with them because it was like why would you do that to yourselves? I understand that you're upset just like I would be upset but you don't destroy your own. I wouldn't have been surprised if a bunch of people would have gotten in their cars and drove out to Simi Valley. Because maybe they were angry about where it happened, but to destroy what belongs to you in your own community and to hurt other neighbors and friends, the people who didn't riot, the people who lived there, that would retire there, and the ones who had small children...maybe you (the rioters) destroyed their car, now that mother can't get herself to work tomorrow and her child to childcare. No thought of what the impact would have on the neighborhood. To me that's uncivilized. I don't care what color you are. I think what they did, although there was a large group of people, is what I call a few who ruined it for many. I feel that it set race relations back for quite awhile. I think people were afraid for quite awhile. It was like…what's the next thing that's going to happen to cause a civil unrest? So I feel that it was the few who really set things back for the many. I would hear people say, "See this is just like they behave." They…they…well once again everybody's in a category or everybody's in a group.

MW: So I am a part of that (they) and they don't even no me. They don't know I was just as scared as they were, or as scared as you were.

KD: Exactly, you didn't want to drive down there. You would drive around. Who in their right mind would want to be in the middle of that? A lot of my heart and fear went out to the innocent. People forget that's a neighborhood. People live there. They have lives. It may not be Bel Air, but it's a neighborhood where there are children and elderly people. And they (the rioters) did that to their own neighborhoods. That's the part that really bothered. But no one thought about what it was going to take to rebuild their community. Nobody stopped and thought about the innocent people who would be hurt. People hit over the head with bricks. I just couldn't believe what I was seeing. It was inhumanity against humanity. I didn't get it. And then when it was all said and done, and things started to calm down, there was the mess, everything that was left that was torn apart, burned down, wrecked cars, and wrecked lives. They didn't care who they hurt. Those people…and I mean "those" people whoever they were out there causing havoc; I'm sure it wasn't all black people but it was those people in that moment that got into that riot…that mentality…and didn't even think that they were destroying what was theirs. And I think that's what hurt me the most because those people out there in the world who look at black people as "those" people are going to judge all black people by what they just did and you have now brought they're brothers and sisters down with them. Unfortunately like I said before the "those" people that I'm talking about are a variety of people, they're not in my life because I don't have that type of mentality and I don't want to hang around those kind of people that have that mentality, but they're people out there that judge "all" and not as individuals. It's a shame that the world is the way it is, but you want to hope and pray that things are improving and that people are starting to see each other for who they are and not the color of their skin, or their religion. I don't want to judge Muslims but sometimes I'm afraid it's human nature but do I group all of them into one category? No I don't.

MW: When Rodney King came out and said, "Can We All Get Along?" How did you feel about that statement?

KD: Well now they make such a joke out of it and they all know that's what Rodney King said. But I wished we could all get along. I don't know why people can't let it go. You said earlier and I think you said it really well, you said, we need to learn how to accept each other's differences." And knowing we're all different isn't that better anyway.

MW: Yes, I don't want anyone to be exactly like me. God made me unique.

KD: Right so that's why we shouldn't judge the book by its cover. I can care less what color your skin is…but I do feel the pain of the black man. I know that that sounds kind of funny but having a mulatto nephew who's gone through a lot of things...I can never walk in his shoes, but I do feel his pain. Those few people (the rioters) made it even harder for him. Because I know there's a lot of people that judge all based on a few. That's where my anger came from. I thought, you stupid ass….are you kidding me? This is what some people live for….just so they can say, "See that's how they are, they're animals." I heard all of this kind of stuff, Michele. They. They.. They..They

MW: I'm sure you've heard all kinds of things but do you hear those kinds of things then, but do you hear that now, today? Do you think things have changed?

KD: Some people are never going to change. I think that over the 20 years that have passed, things have gotten better, I think. For me it's kind of hard because I've always gotten along with people, but I don't hear the tension like during those times during the OJ trial. I think what bothers me today is that you can't talk about certain things. If I talk to a black person at work about another black person at work, unfortunately some people who are black take everything you say as being prejudice. That's still going on, both ways. I want to think we've come so far but we really haven't. I thank God I was raised by the people I was raised by. I went to school with Mexicans fighting in gangs and...I had a very colorful childhood. I get pissed at some of the black leaders we have in this country, not the President, but some of the other black activists in this country who feel like they're doing the black man a service and I think what they do is to continue to try to keep us at odds with each other, keep us divided because they make money. After all they're just people too. It's the people who keep us apart like white supremacists, or Nazis, or anybody who keeps us divided. I'm sure there are people today who still hate the Japanese people for World War II, I don't get it. It would be like you hating me because I'm white because you had slavery in your family. I didn't own anybody. To hold me personally responsible is like…like if I would hold you personally responsible for something bad that happened to me or my family that you had nothing to do with. So when Rodney King said, "Can We all Get Along," I really felt…yes can we just….what is the big deal…what is wrong with people.

MW: And when you say people you mean all people of all races?

KD: I mean everybody. I've always said if someone is not killing someone or breaking any laws, who cares? America is supposed to be this big melting pot of people….let all the people melt in together. But there's already that group that want the rift. They're everywhere. Look at some Muslim people, some of them, all they want to do is kill us. I haven't done anything to them. But it's how they were raised. That mentality. It's the hate Michele, there's so much hate and I don't understand why. So what Rodney said, and it was a very simple line in my mind, "Can We All Get Along?" it's just that simple. Yeah, Can't we? And I don't know Michele if it's ever going to change the way we want it to, in our life time. It's disheartening because I want to be able to talk to my friends whether they're black, Chinese or whatever and know that I can be honest and have an opinion and they're not going to cut my head off when I talk to them; because I would like them to be honest with me. If I do something that annoys you…let me know…talk to me and be honest, please be honest. I don't get defensive about that kind of stuff; I look at it as an opportunity to improve. So when this came up, I thought I'd love to go and talk to Michele because without our differences where would we be? We'd be very unenlightened.

MW: Well Kellie, I'm glad you did volunteer to speak with me and be a part of this project. We had a wonderful lunch and a wonderful conversation. Thank you for your honesty. Who knows maybe one day we will learn to just get along.

Interview w/ Richard Kim

Then: Korean American Electronics Store owner
Now: Korean American Electronics Store owner

MW: Richard, I understand you had a family business in LA during the times of the LA riots?

RK: Yes it was a family business we started in 1976 located at Western and south of 11th st. Between Olympic and Pico. During the time of the Rodney King incident we had moved our first store to Western and 1st and we had a second store on Venice and Westmoreland.

MW: Were your stores in predominantly black communities?

RK: We were in a Hispanic community but most of our customers were across the board, Asians, whites, blacks, Hispanics, it was very diverse.

MW: Did you have any problems with any customers stemming for the verdict or its aftermath?

RK: Since I grew up here, there was no language barrier. I think most of the problems stemmed from cultural and language differences. For example, I was made much more aware of this after the Rodney King incident and after the riots because before the riots there were a couple of things that happened. There was a young lady that had been killed.

MW: LaTasha Harlins

RK: Yes. Although electronics is an upscale business, we did not deal with...well, most of our customers were middle class, so we really didn't have those issues. If our parents owned a liquor store or a convenience store it would have been different. By 1992, we became acutely aware of these incidents happening with the Korean American merchants with African American customers, the conflicts that were happening. There were about 10 different local Korean American store owners in that area and it was called Korean American Electronics Dealers Assoc. which we were part of. In 1992, I was the president of that organization, so as these conflicts were happening, we felt like it was blown up in the media. We met with the Korean American grocers organizations, in their membership were the small convenient store owners in the areas. So I had a chance to meet with some of their members.

MW: Before you go further with that. Were you the president when Latasha Harlins was murdered in 1991 or did you have conversations with these organizations? Did you get a sense that it was worse after the Latasha Harlins incident for the Koreans? Or was it business as usual?

RK: First you have to understand, I do not exemplify a Korean American business person, only because most Korean American businesses were owned by 1st generation Koreans who had a language barrier and one of the biggest issues I've learned is that we didn't have that much interaction with the inner city residents. So as part of the program/association we reached out to other organizations. Riorden wasn't mayor but he had a program for different groups to have dialogue. I was able to sit down with different groups to see what the issues were and I spoke better English than most of the other owners. Some of the core issues were cultural differences. Very basics issues like eye contact. I grew up here so I know you don't stare at someone with an evil eye but it's proper when you're having a conversation to make eye contact. However, in Korea, it's not proper for a store clerk to make direct eye contact because it's like a challenge, so out of respect they look down.

MW: Really?

RK: Not that I would know this so when I heard about these issues, I went back to my parents and said, "What's up with the eye contact." They told me it was improper for a clerk to look someone in the eye because that shows disrespect. Another issue that the residents had was, "they don't speak to me and they don't hand me the change, they (Koreans) put it on the table." So I said again, "What's this about the change?" I was told again by my parents and the Korean community, it's disrespectful for a clerk to give direct eye contact and there's a cultural thing with physical contact. But it was all done out of respect.

MW: That's a big one. Not giving me my change in my hand.

RK: So I was able to go to the African American community and say, "You know, it's not out of disrespect, it's a cultural thing. That's how they were raised." With the younger generation of Koreans it was not that much of an issue; it was really with the older generation. So it was my job to reach out because no one really did anything like this before the riots to see what the issues were. You know the media would come in with the cameras and people would say, (about the Koreans), "They come in (black neighborhoods), they take our money and they drive their nice cars and they don't put back into the community." As far as businesses not giving back to the communities, that's a business decision. Some business reinvests and some do not. However, most of the issues were cultural. The older people were not acclimating themselves fast enough to the community.

MW: What were the issues from the Korean merchant's with African Americans? I'm sure they had some issues also.

RK: One of my close friend's parents owned a store in south central, and they had great relations with some of their immediate neighbors, and some they didn't have good relationships with. Seems only the bad pops up on the media.

As far as the Latasha Harlins incident, I think you just have to have mutual respect and not all merchants were respectful.

MW: So did the older generation complain that the customers came in disrespecting them, by talking loud, or mocking them? What were there complaints?

RK: I think to a certain degree, most of the 1st generation persons, from Korea, they don't speak very loudly, it's a very rigid society, so to come to south central, I think it was a cultural shock for them as well. And for the residents in south central to see the very uptight Koreans, it was a cultural shock for them also. It was a shock to both sides.

 Bottom line is there was a lot of misunderstanding from both sides that no one was really addressing until the riot.

MW: Not until after the riot. Not after the Latasha Harlins incident?

RK: No. It (the Latasha Harlins' incident) happened right after the Rodney King incident. But they didn't start addressing the issues until after the riots. I remember the verdicts like it was yesterday. I was in the store on 1st and Western, it was more upscale. We had an

African American client at the televisions, we had a white person, an Asian person, and we had other people in the neighborhood there. When the verdicts were being read, everybody stopped and watched. When the verdicts were read not guilty, the response was very different; the black person was "I knew it. They were not going to convict a bunch of white cops for beating a black man." He said shrugged his shoulders, "So what else is new." The white guy didn't respond one way or the other, just dead silence. Afterwards, we didn't expect much but then we start seeing things happening on the news. Florence and Normandie and the Reginald Denney beating.

MW: So your store was fine because that (Normandie and Florence incident) happened a couple of hours later?

RK: Yes, because we were close to Hollywood. South central was a world away. But then we were called to a meeting for all of the business owners to come together the next morning. We were to come up with a response as a community. Our response was that we wanted to condemn the verdict to say it wasn't just. So we were preparing this response but by then everything was being destroyed in south central. So the grocers said, we need to go back to our stores. We wanted to give a press release but the news media was covering other things. We still didn't think it would get that bad, we thought it would have been contained. The second day, our store on Western was looted and burned to the ground. That whole corner was burned to the ground.

MW: So how did you feel then?

RK: Not only that, I got a call because I was at the Westmoreland store, my parents were running the one on Western. They called and said, "Richard, you have to get down here, they're shooting and everything." So I left to go to pick them up. As my parents were running away, before I could get there, my mother was shot in the leg. My dad was in his late sixties. One of the neighbors got them into the car and took them to the hospital. So I didn't know where she was. By the time I got there it was total chaos. My friend took pictures of people leaving with boxes of stuff and then within an hour it was torched and burned to the ground. My parents lived in the house behind the store but the fire dept put out the fire so it was OK. The lot is still vacant to this day. My parents still live there today. The people that lived in the neighborhood were very sympathetic to them. I think the people who did that didn't live in that immediate neighborhood.

MW: I didn't learn of all the shootings until I was doing research for this project.

RK: If I was there I would have....you know those were older people. Anyway, I was one of those people that got on the roof, where my other store was located; we boarded up the windows because it had spread all the way to Hollywood area.

MW: So you got some friends and got on the roof of your store?

RK: No. All of the employees showed up. I told them to go home but they wanted to help protect the store and their jobs. We went to the second floor. As looters were coming by, if they saw the store was being protected they'd go on to the stores that weren't being protected.

MW: So were you the group that was on the roofs with the guns?

RK: Yes. We had the guns because if we didn't...but we didn't shoot anybody.

MW: You weren't the ones shooting in the air to scare them away, were you?

RK: No but there was a big furniture store down the street. They took a huge truck and blocked the street and all night we heard gunshots. They were about a block away. There were hundreds of bullet holes in that truck.

MW: That's like a real war.

RK: At that time, I didn't serve in the military, but it really seemed like a scene from the Middle East. It didn't seem like the United States. The 3rd day the army came in. With the looting, burning, shooting, and then the army, it really didn't seem like we were in the United States. So going from, how do we formulate a response to this injustice from a community to literally your mom being shot, one of your businesses being burned down to the ground, and you having to go up and defend it, and it came to a point after the fact, some people said you know what, you should not defend it with guns. You should just let them have it. I think having experienced it, I think they are wrong. It should be your right to defend your property, your livelihood, and your family. We couldn't save the first store but we were able to save the 2nd one because we were on the roof. I don't think I would kill someone for taking something but if they were firing at us, I think it would have been justified to fire back in self defense. Is it worth getting into a firefight to protect your property?

MW: Like you said, not just your property, your livelihood and family.

RK: Yes. I worked hard for this business. It's not the American way to just let someone take it from you. Here 20 years later I feel the same way. I think it's a weak person to say just let them take it. It's not like a robbery standpoint. Like say, someone come in this store now with a gun and say, "Give me your wallet. " I'm going to him my wallet. I'm not going to say, "No," because that would be stupid. But if I have the ability to protect it (the store) from waves of mobs coming, that's a different story. And I don't think I would make a different decision today. If I thought it was a lost cause, I wouldn't put myself in that danger, but if it's a chance to protect my livelihood. Now, if I see someone shooting at my parents, that, I think is self defense too.

MW: Yes, it's self defense. You better not let a gun be around me and I see someone shooting at my mother. After that, (seeing your mother shot and your store being burned down) did you feel any different towards the black community? You can be honest.

RK: To be brutally honest, it was my perspective that it wasn't every black person shooting and rioting, or every Hispanic, it was a small percentage. I don't think it (the riots) could change my perspective of a community as a whole but I think certainly what changed me was that, money isn't everything, to see my mom shot, I think I refocused on family, more like you never know when you're going to go type thing. So I wasn't bitter about the store being burnt down, to focus on that would be very negative. I think, in Korean society you have murderers, burglars, same thing in any society, Having grown up in Pasadena, worked in LA, gone to school in LA, I don't and can't generalize any one group, ethnic or religious group, thinking, oh yeah, there all bad.

MW: What's sad is that does happen way too often.

RK: What I learned a long time ago is... you can't change how other people think. You have ignorant people in Asian communities, ignorant people Hispanic communities; you have ignorant people in every community. So I think what I can change is how I see things. And you can do that one person at a time. You have to get to know a person. It takes effort to get to know the individual and not generalize a whole community, or whole ethnic group, or religious group. Not all Muslims are terrorists. Not every black person is a ...what's the guy's name something football, that beat up Reginald"

MW: Damien "Football" Williams.

RK: Damien "Football" Williams.

MW: I wanted to go through the TV and hurt him.

RK: See coming from an African American woman...I would feel the same way if we had a Korean American do something stupid on television. Because it's an embarrassment on us. So as a whole, you can't judge by the actions of a few individuals.

To reflect on the Ta Kwon Do school. I don't know if you've been there, but it's like the Rainbow Coalition by Jesse Jackson. That school is filled with all ethnicities. Have you been there?

MW: No, but my children were raised in a very diverse community. My son, more than my daughter, has always had a very diverse group of friends. But you know what's sad? As a mother, I had to constantly tell my son who he is in America because he's a black man in America and sometimes you're not treated fairly, he can't be angry at people, but he had to be aware of it. He can't always do everything his friends do because someone will perceive it in a different way. I had to really explain that to him because he'd say, "Why do you guys talk about things like that, we're all one." Because that's how he thinks.

RK: How old is he?

MW: He'll be 25 in February. That's the way he wants to raise his children. No one should think about color. But I had to warn him because I know society. And it's sad but I had to remind him of who he is, not because that's how I want it to be but because that's how society is.

RK: But just to be aware… Probably in my heart I will relate to your son's thinking as well, because I grew up in Sierra Madre, when I was living there it was probably 98% white, so you stuck out. Anybody shade less than white, you stuck out. I like the "color blind" thing. You know there's a bigot in every community, black, Asian, white, Korean, every community, and you can't change that.

MW: You really can't but I think you have to be aware still of who you are...you do. Again, it's sad that I had to tell him that in this day and age. Well, not today, that was when he was a teenager and started driving his car. And he would get stopped.

RK: The whole driving while black thing.

MW: Honestly, my son is very clean-cut. I never allowed him to wear cornrows, I never allowed him to get his ears pierced until he was a little older, and then if he wanted to do that, that was his decisions. But wearing your pants down here, (pointing to below my butt) not happening. So he was very clean cut...and then he'd called me,

"Mom, the police just stopped me and he didn't even give me a ticket, he just asked where was I coming from and going." He'd be all upset. You see that's why I had to let him know so he wouldn't react to a cop. No just keep your cool baby and be calm, and just be cooperative, pray and go on about your business. But if you don't let your children know, I'm sorry as a mother, a black mother my whole job is to protect my children. So I had to make him aware but I also told him I never wanted him to change because I love who he is. He doesn't think about color he's just having a good time and he's so laid back. And that's the way he should be.

MW: Back to your experience.

RK: So the bottom line is this whole experience taught me two things. 1) Money is not everything, value family and close friends, and 2) You can't change how other people perceive you, and you can only change how you perceive other people. Those things are forever etched into my mind. I don't know if I'm a typical Korean American, but I know the younger generation is a lot more open minded. So the biases from the older generation will slowly go away. I do not believe it was a Korean American vs. African American issue. As a matter of fact some black businesses were burned. That "black owned" thing didn't always work.

MW: I think it was a police brutality thing, but a lot of anger came out towards the Korean American community because of the Latasha Harlins incident.

RK: Well, I guarantee you; you didn't see Korean American business people coming out to support the store owner that killed that child. We were, more than anything else, trying to educate people on how to deal with situations like that without going to deadly force. I think the Latasha Harlins case was a wake up call to educate the store owners, to have more outreach to the community. But that was also one store owner, one store, and one incident. Not to defend her or to condemn her, well condemn her for the one wrong decision she made whether the heat of the moment or whatever the case is. Maybe she shouldn't have been minding the store with that kind of issue she had. Like I said, you can't judge the whole community with one incident when there are hundreds of stores.

MW: And that's what's done on all sides.

RK: Yes, that whole racism thing generalizing.

MW: Yes, and that's our problem, we don't sit down and talk to each other and educate each other. Because even for me I didn't know about some of the cultural things that you shared with me this evening.

RK: 20 years later. Oh no, we haven't done a very good job at educating.

MW: I would get very upset when they would put my change on the counter. I thought, you're doing business here but you don't want to touch me?

RK: You experienced that personally?

MW: Yes. And I don't look hard or thuglike in any way.

RK: Oh no, you don't look anything like a thug or any of that.

MW: But I'm not going to yell at you or get an attitude, I will just take my hard earned money elsewhere and I would not go back.

Really, I wouldn't go back. So how many people like me, did the same thing. Because I thought I was being disrespected. See, if we would have had a conversation, I would have known better. So that's really the key and that's why Ontresicia and I agreed, although this is her story, we wanted to have more voices in this book to help educate everybody, because that's really the key in moving forward. Unfortunately, there are a lot of people, I mean you're good, I'm fine, but there are a lot of people that still think the same way.

RK: I think we are both educated and open minded but there are things we do not know about all of each others cultures. We have to have continued dialogue. We have to be able to ask questions if we do not know something.

MW: Yes, without getting your head bit off if you ask.

RK: Yes. We're asking because we want to know.

MW: What did you think of Rodney's statement, "Can we all just get along?"

RK: That can resonate with anybody. My perception was he was put on the spot light and that was the appropriate thing to say.

MW: Well, will end it on that note. Thank you so much for your time and my education of the Korean culture.

Interview with Geoffrey Gill

Then – Director of Music, KJLH
Now – Television and Music Producer

MW: How did you feel when you so Rodney King being Beat?

GG: Hmm... What did I think when I saw Rodney King being beat?

MW: Yes, I mean did you ever wonder; what did he do?

GG: No, I never thought about what had King done because regardless of anything he had done, I was thinking it couldn't have been bad enough to just stand there and beat him, you know....stand there and beat on a man that's trying to protect himself trying to block punches. I had experienced a situation with my brother where the police had done a similar thing. Maybe 5 to 10 years earlier to the King incident. They charge you with resisting arrest while they're beating you and you're reacting by moving your arms around yelling "Oooh ouch." So I felt a connection from that stand point and you know I was glad...I was glad that they got it on tape. I was glad that somebody got it on tape because otherwise he would have ended up in jail and they would have charged him like they charged my brother with battery against the police officers or assaulting a police officer while you're on the ground struggling for your life, that's what they did with my brother. We had a lawsuit and everything but we didn't have cameras....you feel me. So I was happy that they got it on tape. I knew it was something big....I knew it was going to be a defining moment in history.

MW: Do you remember if that incident was announced a lot on the radio?

GG: Hmmm…that was 20 years ago, yeah, I was what 23?

MW: Yeah, you were a youngster.

GG: Yeah, I was a youngster I had a lot on my mind back then, I saw it but it's not like I was responsible, I wasn't an activist but it was part of the news every morning, people talked about it a lot. Carl Nelson, he did the morning show and they would talk about it because that was their job from a journalistic stand point to document. So I would hear about it. But at the time it wasn't my position, I was flash and music and fun.

MW: So a year later when you, your station, received the verdicts…take me to that day. What happened?

GG: I was doing afternoons at the time, which was the 2pm to 6pm shift, and right around 3:45pm is when they read the verdicts on TV and the whole world was watching, not guilty, not guilty, not guilty, not guilty…WOW! It's like wait…did you see what happened? We got you on tape…you could see it…you know it was just as obvious as Michael Jackson took propofol, you're guilty. Some things you just see automatically. But to see them found not guilty was insightful. It was complete injustice…made you feel very um…you know….polarized…you felt black…you felt very cheated.

MW: What do you mean you felt black?

GG: When I say black…you felt black…like we're sitting out here right now in Valencia and we're the only two black people. I feel black out here right now. I felt discriminated against.

MW: You personally?

GG: Me personally. I felt my entire race had just been...an injustice had been committed against us. I'm sure that everybody that was African American or anybody who had any common sense from other races of people, felt something was wrong. The justice system had failed. So I had another break, we'd talk about 5 or 6 times an hour so I opened the mic. I don't know what I said but I said something like, WOW the verdicts are out and....I went on a rant because I was emotional and I shared my feelings for about a minute or two or three. I don't know because it's all a blur, but I remember my supervisor, the program director, came walking in and he took his hand and went across his neck saying, "Stop. Cut."

MW: To you?

GG: Yeah to me because it was too personal, so he kept saying, "cut, cut." So I looked at him and I said, "OK." Then I talked for another minute to minute and a half then I cut. Then he said, "Don't say anything else about it. The media went out and everybody needs to lay low and calm down". It was like a stick of dynamite and the fuse had been lit.

MW: Did he think you would incite something?

GG: No. He just didn't want the station to take a position and be that personal. You know, I don't know what he thought but whatever I was doing was what needed to be done. (He laughs) In my opinion, I was placed in a situation like, what's the guys name during the 65 riots....he said, "Burn Baby Burn" (Magnificent Montague) I'm fast forwarding from '65 to '92 and I'm that guy. So I'm sitting there 24 years old and I'm on the air. And it got crazy. The next few minutes it was crazy, phones were buzzing and blinking, everybody was calling, phones lines were lit up and people were calling in saying they should be guilty. "I know. I know calm down," I was telling the callers. So I'm talking to everybody and I'm feeling the energy because you really have a connection with the people with 10 phone lines and they're on fire. And the red line, you know every station has a red line, the red line was the traffic lady, we have traffic that comes in from an outside source. She said, hey there's a disturbance at Florence and Normandie but they don't want us to report on it.

MW: She was the Newsperson, the traffic newsperson?

GG: Yeah for traffic and she said, they don't want me to say anything about it. But people are getting unruly over there....there's violence and all that, but they don't want us to say anything.

MW: What they? Who was she talking about?

GG: They, meaning the authorities, police or whoever. So don't say anything. As I'm talking to people on the phone, my sense of responsibility...I felt like I didn't want anybody to get hurt. Honestly.

MW: Right of course not.

GG: I got friends and my listeners, so I said "Look everybody needs to calm down, everybody just needs to relax, OK. So I understand that...they don't want me to tell you but...there's a disturbance on Florence and Normandie. I don't want anybody to go over there because I don't want you to get hurt...I care about you....I'm Geff Gill, I love you...and I want you all to calm down."

MW: There's that radio voice.

GG: Just calm down and relax. We're going to fight this fairly, there's no reason for this to get out of hand. We all know what happened to Reginald Denny over there. I remember getting phone calls after that, from people, you know that can't resist when you say don't do something or don't go somewhere....what do people do? They go.

MW: There were rumors that Denny and Fidel they didn't listen to....you know our stations...so I don't know what stations they listened to but they obviously weren't warning people like KJLH.

GG: They got caught up in the wrong place at the wrong time. Whatever station they listened to, I'm sure they heard the verdict but they didn't have any idea. They didn't know the magnitude of it. But if they weren't listening to the radio maybe on the CB radio you missed it. You got caught in the wrong place at the wrong time and it was sad.

MW: So the hours went on and you were supposed to be there from 2:00pm to 6:00pm so what was it like, the feel of the station?

GG: We were right in the center of the war zone. The riots happened right around us. We were on Crenshaw in between King and Rodeo right next to Los Angelus funeral home. I was sitting right there and I had a birds eye view of Crenshaw blvd right out the window. That was our advantage right at street level. You could see the energy in the street plus it was rush hour so cars were right out in front in the neighborhood. We were just put in that situation. I think we won the Peabody award for our broadcast and our coverage of the riots. We became 24 hr coverage for information and news because that was your sense of responsibility, to be there for the community. So for 24 hours that's what we did. I ended up being on the air until about midnight. Rico (another radio personality) came in after me and took over but the reason I was there so long is because after the riots broke out, no one could get to the station.

MW: Oh, I didn't hear that much about disturbances on Crenshaw.

GG: Oh you didn't hear about, well I'll tell you about it because I was there. While listeners were calling me telling me about where the rioting was taking place, what was going on and I was getting feeds from AP (Associated Press). I watched building after building on Crenshaw getting raided some caught on fire right across the street. People were just taking whatever they could…robbing. It was a place called Thai pings on the corner, it was a bar, they raided that. "Thai Pings" sat no more. The liquor store, they got the liquor store. Next to the liquor store was the TV repair shop…they raided the TV "repair" shop…and I remembered being on the air saying hey they're over here taking "broken" TVs, those TVs are broken people…Stop! You know what I mean… (he laughed) but they didn't care. It was complete chaos it was off the hook and we're sitting here in the middle of it and I'm watching the whole thing across the street. People just grabbing stuff; carrying stuff out like no big deal. My friends were calling me saying they're at Fedco….Fedco was being robbed people were taking everything; they were running out with computers and printers.

MW: What did they do; ambush the Fedco staff?

GG: Just ambushed them. I heard the people got so strong they were carrying computers (back then computers were much larger than now) because the adrenaline was just running through them. I heard a white guy was at Fedco, maybe an employee, and a black guy said

"You ...you...carry my stuff to the car." The white guy said I don't want to carry that stuff....The guy made him carry his stuff to the car. The 7Eleven (a convenience store) on Stocker and Overhill...complete shambles, the only thing left was the ATM. I really felt like I had missed out on what was going on because I was on the air. I could only report what people were calling in telling me.

MW: Weren't the buildings over there on Crenshaw mainly black owned businesses?

GG: Well, they skipped over the black owned businesses. They were very meticulous they knew which ones were and which ones weren't and if you weren't (black) you were going to be targeted. I'm sure some of the black ones (stores) got mixed up in it.

I remember leaving the station, I used to drive a jeep, maybe around midnight, it was Marshall Law (Military rules in emergency situations) at that point the guards were in the streets. Because we were in the center, there were fires all around, I was trying to get to Studio City where I lived, safely. The guard had a machine gun just standing on the street, I said, "can I go this way?" he didn't say a word he looked straight ahead. I said hmmm... he doesn't want to talk to me. I turned and drove up Rodeo, there was a Shell station on the corner, it was being raided; people were pumping gas, you could pump before paying back then. So I drove by and tried to hang a left on Crenshaw and it explodes...Boom! The whole convenience store on the lot with the Shell gas station...Boom! It's on fire. I'm like WOW! It was a war zone. It felt like I was driving in what you would see in World War II. So I'm in the jeep and I'm driving zigzagging in the street because people were all in the middle of the street, complete anarchy and then I pass by the Arco gas station on Jefferson and it's on fire. I was driving through a war zone. I finally hit the 10 freeway and went towards the 405 freeway and said, "Whew! I made it! And that was that experience and it continued for the next couple of days. I went back to work the next day. Oh yeah, that's where I wanted to be. We had a lot to do and people were pulling long air shifts and we were talking the whole time. We were constantly interviewing people, the mayor, dignitaries... trying to cool everybody down... then Rodney King comes on the air and says, "Can We Just Get Along? That was profound. Can We Just Get Along?

MW: Yeah, what did you think about that?

GG: He paused for a minute...Thinking back, Can We Just Get Along? Come on Rodney.... (He looked at me) Can We Just Get Along? I felt that he felt that he was sorry he was in the middle of it all, and his humanity, at that point came out and he said those words. He was the one person that could have calmed everybody. It's like I'm not out fighting and I'm the one they did this to. Can We All Get Along? So I think the media came and gave him a chance to say something, to calm it down and um...those are the words that ring out to this day – Can We All Just Get Along? You know, now those words could have had like a reverse reverberation because they could have just gotten along when they pulled Rodney over – they could have just gotten along then. So it wasn't just about that the violence kicked in it was can WE ALL GET ALONG? If we were all just getting along, this never would have happened in the first place. So that was kind of the feeling I got from it. His voice shook as he said it, at that point, I think everybody just kind of stopped and said, look what's going on, you know. But I think it's something that had to happen.

MW: Oh Really?

GG: I think at that point, when you push people so far – something like that had to happen. It was time to take notice. It was sad that it ruined a lot of businesses and changed a lot of lives. People were hurt and killed but I think it happens in every revolution…like it's happening now. Around the world people feel like they've been abused…they feel held down…so that is part of the progress and the process. That unfortunately was one that had to take place…it was inevitable.

MW: Looking back now as a grown man you think it had to take place?

GG: Well, I'm not justifying or condoning the violence. I'm just saying that it was inevitable…something had to happen.

MW: The explosion.

GG: Yes the Explosion had to happen…if they could have gotten to the police officers…if they (the police) were walking down the street they would not have made it. If you've ever had someone do you wrong personally and you wish you could get your hands on them. If I was a Jackson right now and I was just feet away from the guy that gave my brother, son, uncle, father, propofol, I'd find it hard to restrain myself from at least trying to choke the shit out of him. You follow me? So when you have that pent up in you and there's nothing that you can do…from your own voice…I think that's what happened. A lot of people had the same emotion going on at the same time and anytime that happens...I mean you can get a crowd together and start a riot yourself anywhere...if you get them motivated on the same thing. So everyone was just polarized in that condition and it was bound to explode....it was just bound to happen. Like if you put stress on any situation, too much stress on it and it's going to snap...everyone just snapped. It's like well, how much do you think we're going to take.

MW: Do you think it had a lot to do with the Latasha Harlins incident as well? Because those things happened back to back.

GG: People were still reeling from Latasha Harlins.

MW: Seeing her picture reminded me of my daughter.

GG: You saw your daughter...you saw yourself.

MW: I thought we were still steaming but I don't think I was steaming like a man.

GG: Yeah, It's a whole another thing when you've been taken advantage of as a man, your testosterone and manhood has been challenged. You're dealing with your women and you have to stand up for them...your woman is hurt...your momma is hurt. You identified directly with Latasha Harlins; my brother – Rodney King same person. Then you go back and look at slavery, and look at all the oppression that has taken place, they shot Dr. Martin Luther King and you start thinking of all these things and it's like, I've had enough. Today is my day and I'm going to go off today....whatever happens today is going to happen. Does it make it right? Umm that's not the point....at that instance...that's not the point. Police officers driving around trying to subdue the action, if you will, but they were like I'm cool, I'm not even getting out of my car...you guys are doing a little bit too much for me. You got to let that moment happen...we had that moment and we look back on it and I'm ashamed of the fact that it was our communities that got burned down. I know the people in Orange County and Beverly Hills, we wouldn't have made it to Beverly Hills, were probably saying, "hey they're burning their own stuff down; look at those dummies," and that's cool, that's what they have to say and I get that. That's the sad part about it but what are going to do? If we drive to Beverly Hills and burn Beverly Hills up. Well, no that was not going to happen because that would have taken time and premeditation, gasoline, and by that time the people would have cooled off and realized the error of their ways...so it was the moment.

MW: That's right. It wasn't premeditated it was a reaction at the moment, for some.

GG: No it wasn't premeditated. It was the same reaction I had when I opened the mic on the air. I'm upset and guess what...I've got a microphone...and I know people feel the way I do and I'm going to talk about it, right now. What? I'm going to not say something?

MW: Yeah, you couldn't ignore something that big.

GG: No you couldn't ignore it. I look back on it and I don't know if I perpetuated the situation or caused people to do things that they shouldn't have (Laugh) but I tell you I felt a sense of camaraderie, that I'll never forget. Everybody was on the same page for one minute and we all came together and said, "No More! No More. You can not do this to me. You can not do this to my brother. You can not do this any more .And if you do ....guess what? We're all upset and you're going to have to fight us all." And everybody joined together for that moment and said hey, No More! No More.

MW: WOW!

GG: At that moment I'm going to go out here and protest and this is my cause for today. Danny Bakewell came out, Magic Johnson, Jesse Jackson, anyone who had any kind of sense of black pride. They were the role models at that time, they all came together. It wasn't about let's get together and riot...it was about let's get together and send this voice out and say, No More! You know those people fight in their own way and people in the streets in poverty, that don't have a microphone, that don't have a way to complain, and don't have money for lawyers, they fight in their own way, and they needed to speak. They spoke on that day and they said, "No More." There were some that took advantage, you know, I'm going to go get me some "stuff," I need some stuff...Stuff is going to make me feel better. You feel bad, get some ice cream, feel down, some people go to food, or run to whatever's going to make them feel better, sex, drugs, whatever and that day it was shopping...it was free shopping everything is free. I have mixed emotions.

MW: Yes. You did tell the people where they could go.

GG: I was just reporting what I heard.

MW: Your intentions were to keep them from those places.

GG: My intentions were to report what was going on. The Koreans were shooting on top of the roofs. That was in Korean town they were like, 'okay soul brother, run over here, you going back limping'.

We didn't get back to normal programming until about 5 or 6 days later. Was I wrong?

MW: No you were doing your job you were suppose to report what was going on and that helped people like me. Because when I got off work, I was working at Cedars Sinai hospital, I was listening to the radio and if you were saying this and that is happening over here or over there, I was staying away from that area. So I don't think you were wrong at all because I needed you to guide me and I'm sure there were others like me that didn't want to get caught in the middle of the rioting. So I needed you; so you were right and I thank you now for myself and on the behalf of all those people you helped get home that evening safely.

GG: (He laughs at my gratitude.) I feel better...I was the Chick Hearns of the streets.

From the words of Dr, King "If a man has not found something he's willing to die for, then he's not fit to live."

MW: Thank you for sharing your personal experiences and feelings on this topic. We'll end right here with that great quote from a great man.

www.ingramcontent.com/pod-product-compliance
Lightning Source LLC
Chambersburg PA
CBHW032052090426
42744CB00005B/188